My Story:
The COVID-19 Vaccine
and
Brain Damage

Dear Donna,
Thank you for me!
your support! So nice
to have met you!
Blessings,
Lynette

4 C. Lynette Milakovich

Cover Design: Best in Business Publishing, LLC
or Book Design & Formatting: Best in Business Publishing, LLC
r: Best in Business Publishing, LLC

by: Best in Business Publishing, LLC
Congress Cataloging – Publication Data has been applied

3336209495
N THE UNITED STATES OF AMERICA.

In Memory Of

The two children of my friends and others who died
suddenly, those who took their lives, and the many who
died from conditions acquired from the COVID-19 vaccine.

Acknowledgements

My dear husband Dan, I want to thank you and tell you how much I love you for your steadfast dedication through the most trying time of our marriage. You went through hell with me and witnessed the most frightening times. You easily could have given up and walked away, but you didn't. I'll be forever grateful to you. You are my rock!

Thank you, my dear son Bryce, who saw me deteriorate almost every day not knowing what was happening and feeling helpless. You tried so hard to reassure me and support me in your usual kind and strong ways.

I am ever so grateful to you, my daughter Kelli, three months pregnant, working, studying for your CPA exam, for dropping everything at home and flying out of Hawaii at a moment's notice, taking charge, and intuitively knowing what I needed. My gratitude extends to you, Jeff, the best son-in-law ever, for supporting Kelli as she came to take care of me.

Dr. Marivik Villa, thank you for your courage in recognizing the vaccine-injured. You gave me the tests that allowed a diagnosis of injury from the COVID-19 vaccine and validated all of my symptoms. You were the catalyst that got me to Florida where I healed.
I will always be grateful to you.

Thank you, Aviv Clinic, for saving my life. I cannot express in words the gratitude I have for all Aviv personnel and founders of this amazing place of healing. The validation and support every step of the way through treatment and beyond is profound. After numerous doctors' visits trying to get better to no avail, Aviv Clinics ordered tests that showed the injury to my brain and then healed me. The personnel at Aviv Clinic are the most phenomenal group of people I have ever encountered. And I couldn't have asked for more supportive and fun dive mates. I love you all and thank you for a renewed and wonderful life I never knew was possible.

My gratitude goes out to React19 for supporting the hundreds of thousands of vaccine-injured. Brianne Dressen and Dr. Joel Wallskog spearheaded a most amazing organization to help others injured because of their own injuries. React19 board member Julia Marks, thank you for your support and trust in me to help with the injured. The frontline doctors and nurses who are willing to be truthtellers and giving of their time supporting the injured are in a class by themselves and are gifts to us outside of the broken medical system.

"One of the most important things that the COVID vaccine injured need is they need recognition. It all starts with recognition. Until people can see that this is a problem, nothing is going to be able to be addressed. If you can't see it, then you don't know that it needs to be fixed. They're invisible. Those people that are walking around with this screaming in their head 24-7, you're not even going to suspect that the person you just passed by is enduring an unbelievable hell every single day of their life."

Brianne Dressen, Co-Founder React19
"The Unseen Crisis: Vaccine Stories You Were Never Told"

Caveat

The word "vaccine" is used throughout this book, although "The Centers for Disease Control and Prevention (CDC) altered the definition of 'vaccine'" on September 1, 2021, "because of concern that the definition didn't apply to COVID-19 vaccines…" from "A product that stimulates a person's immune system to produce immunity to a specific disease, protecting the person from that disease," to "A preparation that is used to stimulate the body's immune responses against diseases." (Stiebers, 2021)

"Where You've Seen mRNA Techniques at Work. The vaccines made by Pfizer-BioTech and Moderna use mRNA to fight COVID-19. When these vaccines were rolled out, it was the first time mRNA was used on humans in vaccine technology." (Google, March 10, 2024)

Foreword
By Dr. Mohammed Elamir

The brain and body do not discriminate what hurts it. If you've been in a car accident, did you notice or care the color of the other car that hit you? No! The same goes for injury to the brain. Whether it is a stroke, traumatic brain injury from a fall, a virus like Covid, or a mal-response to a vaccine, injury is injury.

The key to healing an injury is to understand the "how" and "why" the injury is happening and, of course, figuring out the right way to remedy it. That is the philosophy of the Aviv Clinic and by all who practice medicine at Aviv. It is imperative to use state-of-the-art diagnostic assessments to understand the process of injury to the brain and body. This along with a scientifically backed and researched treatment protocol is how we can heal injury. This includes a revolutionary approach to an existing technology, hyperbaric oxygen therapy (HBOT). HBOT involves breathing 100% oxygen under pressure. At Aviv Clinic this is administered in custom-built hyperbaric oxygen suites, which allows for a Nobel Prize-winning concept of fluctuating oxygen to trigger a regeneration mode in the body. There is nothing more powerful than having the body heal itself. It just takes the right trigger and environment to do so.

Along with the powerful physiologic healing of the HBOT protocol, the right disciplinary medical team helps guide and amplify the results. Often in the world of medicine, communication and teamwork is disjointed, making care inefficient or even dangerous. Imagine having your doctors, therapists, and clinicians communicating together with you and each other all under one roof. This model at Aviv Clinic allows for instant and meaningful results.

Human nature is inherently good. As a species we are collectively social and caring. We often do the right things, but we can't always rely on this when it comes to individualized medical care. Knowing what and how to ask the right questions is critical to getting the care you need. Lynette came through the Aviv Clinic and experienced the right individualized care.

The COVID-19 pandemic has changed the world in many ways. In the middle of it we all prayed and hoped for it to end so life could go back to normal. Of course, now that the acute pandemic is over, a new pandemic is upon us. Long COVID is becoming more and more recognized, whether from the virus itself or inappropriate responses from the vaccine. Many people around the world are suffering and looking for answers. In this book you will follow Lynette on her life journey through Long COVID. Whether you are suffering from Long COVID or not, all will be able to understand and empathize with the journey. I have been fortunate to meet Lynette early in her journey and have been mesmerized by her recovery. She is truly an amazing human being, and I hope you enjoy reading her story.

A Note about Lynette's Brain Scans
from Dr. Elamir

Often people undergo imaging of the brain like a CT scan or MRI. These standard scans evaluate structure, but not necessarily function. Scans like a functional MRI (MRI) or SPECT offer more of a functional look. They can tell us how the brain cells are metabolizing at that moment. This is helpful for patients with stroke, traumatic brain injury, and Long COVID.

In Lynette's scans we see her original SPECT scans observing the brain from different angles. The colors represent levels of metabolic activity. Blue is the lowest level of activity signaling damage. Green represents brain cells that aren't working at normal function. Yellow means average function. Orange/red/pink/white is the best level of function. The first row of scans shows Lynette's pre-treatment scan which shows most damage in the front and sides of the brain. The second row is her SPECT scans taken over a year after she finished treatment. The areas of blue and green have significantly improved going up to more metabolically active color levels. Even the normal parts of her brain show significant improvement. She had improvements up to 20% in areas of the brain responsible for memory, attention, language, mathematical ability, and motor function. The SPECT scans were a great way to diagnose the damage to her brain that was responsible for her symptoms and an excellent way to clinically show the improvements from the HBOT treatment.

Brain Scans

September 12, 2022

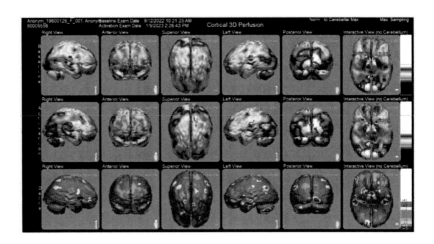

January 8, 2024

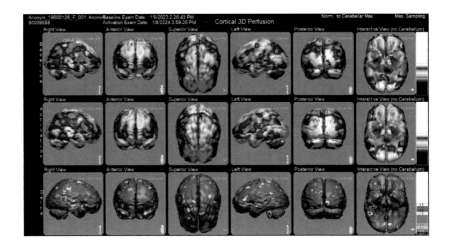

Introduction

It was a day in September of 2022, the day I had been anxiously waiting for two weeks following the pre-assessment testing at Aviv Clinic in Florida. As I followed Dr. Alvarez into the small, brightly lit room with only four chairs, a round table, and a large wall-mounted computer screen, my eagerness was growing as I was about to learn of the test results and hopefully the reason for the total hell I had been experiencing the last year and a half.

Before the testing, I had met with Dr. Alvarez in his office at the Aviv Clinic. He was an older, white-haired gentleman with glasses and a quirky smile. I immediately felt as if I were in the presence of a beloved grandfather with his friendliness and light-hearted sense of humor. I explained my many symptoms and expressed my deep-down gut feeling that they were caused by the COVID-19 vaccine because of the sudden and intense symptoms within a week of receiving the second Pfizer shot and a recent diagnosis of COVID-19 vaccine injury from my new primary care physician in Florida. Tests also showed no antibodies for the COVID virus. The doctor nodded in agreement and explained that the symptoms were typical from what he had seen over the time of the pandemic and was knowledgeable about the similarities of the long-term effects from both the virus and the vaccine.

***

From the published studies by Aviv Clinic's Dr. Shai Efrati and Dr. Amir Hadanny of the treatment protocol of long COVID, treatment focuses on the specific area of the brain that is damaged, but Aviv's treatment helps heal all cells of the body. (*Scientific Reports – Hyperbaric oxygen therapy improves neurocognitive functions and symptoms of post-COVID condition: randomized controlled trial – Abstract.)* As we Aviv Long COVID clients learned from each other while in treatment, the symptoms are the same or similar, whether from the virus or the vaccine. The focus of Aviv is healing the damaged areas of the body and brain, not necessarily the cause. Unfortunately, the Centers for Disease Control does not include the COVID-19 vaccine as a cause within its "Long COVID" definition. (*CDC.gov; Updated July 20, 2023.*)

***

Dr. Alvarez opened my pre-assessment booklet. The buildup of my hope of finally having an answer to my nightmare was coming to fruition, invalidating the labels that had been placed on me by many doctors, some family members, and a few friends who kept telling me I was bipolar, crazy, menopausal, and having a nervous breakdown.

The blood tests were basically normal, which was not a surprise since all my blood tests, except for the thyroid tests and blood pressure readings, were always in the normal range. My chest x-ray was clear. The brain MRI showed nothing of particular significance. The cognitive performance tests revealed above average range for my age, even with the loss I was experiencing with cognition, attention, organization, focus, and emotion.

Dr. Alvarez then directed me to a colorful picture of my brain on the computer screen. It was the results of the SPECT scan, a test that measures brain function.

He said, "Here's how we know what's happening

with you. You see these blue forks here in the front part of your brain? This is the area that is damaged, and that's how we know you have Long COVID."

Finally!! I knew it all along!! It was proof of what I had known deep down in my gut. It validated what I had been expressing to people who had been gaslighting me.

Dr. Alvarez also pointed out that the damage continued into the basal ganglia in the brain which coincided with the tremors and convulsions and the lack of emotion.

***

I had never really understood how the brain controls every aspect of our being. For twelve years I watched my mother's behavior from Alzheimer's disease change from being able to engage in our normal cultural environment to the inability to recognize her own husband or knowing where to relieve herself. I witnessed her changes without being able to see inside her brain to know the direct source of the changes. After the frightening journey of experiencing the inability to function normally within myself, I now understand the connection to the functions of the brain. Changes in the brain can happen to any of us. No one is immune.

The following is my harrowing story of losing myself over a year-and-a-half period and the forces I endured before finding a place where I was embraced, validated, and healed of the brain damage that was caused by the COVID-19 vaccine.

Chapter 1

It was the morning of April 7, 2021, when I awoke with a loud buzzing in my head.

Wow, how strange! What is this noise in my head?

It reminded me of when as a child the tv stations would shut down late at night and be replaced by a screen of fuzziness.

As I rose out of bed at my usual early hour, I dressed to go to my morning physical training with five other women in a friend's garage a few miles away. When I arrived and greeted my workout friends, I told them about the constant buzzing. One gal mentioned tinnitus, something I had heard about from a prospective juror while reporting a criminal trial. I was hoping that wasn't the case as the juror expressed his hesitancy to sit on the jury because of the inability to concentrate with such a condition. It sounded torturous.

After the workout I drove home, took a bath, and continued on as if it were a normal day. I was probably scheduled to report a deposition. Ever since the shutdowns due to the pandemic and California's protocols, depositions were conducted via Zoom, so I was working from home. After a 37-year career in the courtroom, I enjoyed the freedom of being able to work on my own time and continue doing a job in which I loved and flourished for most of my adult life.

The job of a court reporter can be very intense and emotional at times, especially when hearing victims' and even defendants' stories. It is a job that few are privy to being a part of and gaining insight into the realities of life with the variety of witnesses, physical evidence, and the drama that occurs. It is also quite an education to hear from expert witnesses on every subject that comes through a courtroom, which is almost every aspect of life. To be certified as a court reporter, one does not need a college degree. Yet to be a court reporter requires a lot of self-discipline, stamina, intelligence, and organization to get through two-plus years of concentrated study, a two-day state examination, and an intense job which accounts for its substantial earnings.

As the day wore on, I noticed a feeling through my whole body that I would later describe such as pins and needles, overactivity of the nerves, or nerves on fire. Little did I know what the next almost two years would hold for me.

***

When it came time to retire that evening, I didn't have my usual drowsiness. I had always been a good sleeper and loved my sleep. Being a health nut, I knew sleep was a key factor to a healthy life. I was an early-to-bed-early-to-rise sleeper which meant usually 7:00 p.m. to 4:30 a.m. I enjoyed crawling into my comfy bed and watching "Two and A Half Men" or a true crime story (I never got enough of the courtroom!), reading a favorite spiritual book, or just being in silence and talking with God and then drifting off to sleep. My friends would tease me about going to bed before the sun went down or leaving a party just to sleep.

One friend would say, "You can sleep when you die!"

When it came to the evening of April 7, 2021, as I laid my head on the pillow trying to wind down, and the buzzing became intense. I tried relaxing and meditating techniques I taught as a yoga and meditation instructor. My body nor my mind would relax. It could not shut down.

Dan, my husband, came to bed a few hours later and I was still awake with no feeling of drowsiness.

"Honey, I haven't been able to fall asleep at all!" I said with frustration.

"You mean you haven't slept at all?" he asked.

"No. And the buzzing won't stop."

"You'll fall asleep. Just relax," he said trying to reassure me.

He pulled up the covers and soon fell asleep. I lay awake all night trying different positions while doing breathing exercises and yoga nidra.

As the morning came near, my anxiety piqued.

How am I going to be able to function with no sleep? Is this going to happen again tonight and every night?

This would be the beginning of my search for the many natural sleep aids and psychiatric medications that this journey would take me.

***

The next day and days beyond I went to the local health food stores shopping for natural sleep supplements. I read a book on overcoming insomnia naturally that was written by a pharmacist who was a witness at an earlier deposition in which I was the reporter, and I gave her regimen a try plus anything else that was a natural sleep aid. Nothing worked. Nothing gave me that drowsy feeling that one normally needs to fall asleep. I must have been getting some shuteye here and there or I would not have been able to minimally function during the day. I just couldn't pinpoint when. I never felt tired during the day.

What is happening to me? Why do I feel like electricity is running through my body from head to toe? And why the general fogginess that I am experiencing?

I scoured the internet for anything I could find regarding sleep and what brought on all these strange symptoms. I had some leftover Xanax prescribed to me to relax when I flew. I did not want to become addicted to a benzodiazepine, but it would become something that I would take as a last resort.

In the meantime, one of my workout buddies gave me some Ambien and told me to just take a fourth of a pill. I did what she suggested, and, sure enough, I fell asleep and slept a good six to seven hours. But when I awoke, got out of bed, and went outside as usual to listen to the birds sing, I could feel a deep sadness, what I had known as depression. I took the Ambien a few more nights, and each morning the depression had grown to a depth of total despair. I knew I could no longer continue with this medication.

***

What is happening with me? What caused all these symptoms that had come on so suddenly? Wait! What about the vaccine? That was March 31, 2021, just a week before everything began! Could that be the cause? I've never felt anything like this before! I heard that the vaccine wasn't necessarily ripe for distribution, but the pharmaceutical companies and the government would never allow something that wasn't positively safe and effective as they've advertised and promoted for the benefit of humanity.

I did not want to believe the COVID-19 vaccine was the cause, but it was always in the back of my mind until the moments came with evidence and proof that it definitely was.

Chapter 2

Dan and I lived in Southern California below the foothills of Mt. Baldy. We were married in 1984 and decided to raise our children in the suburb of Upland. Most winters held the most picturesque view of snow-capped mountains and blue skies on a sunny day. I spent a lot of time as a child and an adult hiking, camping, and skiing in Mt. Baldy. We lived between the two metropolitan cities of Los Angeles and San Bernardino in what is called the Inland Empire (IE), so we were surrounded by mountains.

The downside to living in the IE is the smog in the summertime that was captured within the mountain ranges. When I was a child, I would go outside to play until it became too difficult to breathe, so I would take a one to two-hour nap to be able to easily breathe again. When landing at Ontario International Airport, passengers can see the thick blanket of dirt below the plane as it descends into the large brown cloud to land.

Growing up in California was nice as we body-surfed at Newport Beach and played in the snow at Mt. Baldy or Big Bear. I was born in Pomona and grew up in Claremont where I went to the public schools except for three years in elementary school at St. Paul's Episcopal in Pomona. My grandparents lived in Pomona, so I spent quite a lot of time with them. In September we loved to go to the L.A. County Fair in Pomona.

California was changing steadily until around 2014 when Proposition 47 passed which allowed for petty thefts with priors to no longer be classified as felonies but, rather, as misdemeanors, no matter how many times the subject had stolen. I worked in the courtroom and was well-informed about the laws, especially in the criminal field. My heart dropped the morning I found out the proposition passed because I knew that would be the beginning of soaring crime rates.

How could this happen? Why would a majority vote for such a law? But who could blame the citizens of California? It was deceitfully named "The Safe Neighborhood and Schools Act."

The rationale behind Proposition 47 was that drug addicts naturally steal for their habits, so instead of the money being put into the courts, jails, and prisons, it would be put into rehabilitation. Both commercial theft and residential theft became rampant. "The aftermath of Prop 47 revealed a surge in overdose deaths due to a lack of mandatory substance-abuse treatment, a surge of shoplifting brought about by diminished consequences, and a failure to address recidivism among repeat offenders." *(GrowSF.org; August 31, 2023.)* We have all seen news clips of mobs going into commercial businesses and grabbing hundreds of dollars or more merchandise and leaving the store. High-end stores in San Francisco's main shopping area closed and are left empty.

Homelessness also greatly increased in Los Angeles and San Francisco counties expanding into the surrounding areas.

Our costs of utilities, gas, and food increased up to 300 percent in the last six months we lived in California.

For all of the above-stated reasons, we decided to leave the once beautiful state in which we both were raised.

***

I learned of a 55+ community called The Villages in Central Florida from a friend with whom I had worked in the early 80's who moved there. The lifestyle of The Villages is something to behold in the later years with lots of golf courses, pickleball courts, bands playing every night in the squares, and any kind of hobby or club one can imagine. The gorgeous landscaping and varying prices of homes make it an affordable place for any retiree.

Dan and I had planned on moving to Florida after we retired if our daughter Kelli and her husband Jeff got stationed back in Jacksonville at Mayport Naval Base. They had met at Mayport while both in the Navy, and they were married in St. Augustine in July 2019. Dan and I had visited quite a bit for six years when Kelli was in the Navy and enjoyed the clear skies, beautiful greenery, and lots of waterways. We found the southern hospitality to be heartfelt. Plus, the cost of living was so much less.

As life would have it, Kelli and Jeff did get stationed in Jacksonville, and we moved to The Villages but not without the battle with my health. It was divine intervention that brought me to Aviv Clinics in The Villages. It is the place that saved my life, only one of three of its kind in the world.

Chapter 3

As time went on since the day the sudden symptoms presented themselves, I tried to keep my same lifestyle of working out, walking with my closest friend, working on Zoom, teaching yoga, household duties, and engaging socially, but these tasks became less and less as time went on. The yoga class that I had been teaching every Wednesday at 10:00 a.m. I gave up because of the lack of sleep, plus I lost my skill to organize yoga poses and I was having trouble remembering the verbiage.

I tried to continue my high-intensity interval training (HIIT) workouts on my own time at the gym, having to pace myself and rest in between workouts due to the chest pressure and fast heartbeats. In 2022 I finally quit going to the gym.

I just can't stand this anymore! The loud music bangs in my head and the chest pressure and heart rate are out of control! I'll just take walks outside instead.

On my walks in the mornings, I would put YouTube on my phone and listen to Joel Osteen, Wayne Dyer, Louise Hay, and lots of other inspirational audio to give me hope that one day I would be healed. I was feeling more and more desperate.

Another symptom that occurred was a drop in weight of twenty pounds over a two-month period. I was already in great shape. I would have liked to lose five pounds but not like this. Veins were popping out of my arms and hands, and my whole body just looked bony. I was eating plenty but could not stop the weight loss.

I feel as if I am dying! I look so haggard and skinny. I feel like I've aged ten years. This is not right at my age!

Bryce was a police officer in the same town that we lived, so he would stop by our house almost every day to check on me. He was stunned with my weight loss and called Kelli immediately with concern.

"Kelli, Mom is so skinny! She looks like she's dying!"

He witnessed my deterioration and increasing tremors and constant agitation over the many months.

***

My closest friend of 25 years and I continued our twice-a-week walks, unless she was out of town visiting her granddaughter. Kathy was an attractive woman who was around my age with a strong personality and with whom I loved and cared. We shared many beautiful times in the past talking about spirituality and philosophy, had a lot of laughs and tears, and gave support to one another the best each could.

Our friendship seemed to be changing within the past four or five years, and things finally came to a head at the beginning of 2021. We were working on continuing our friendship, although our walks were unusually uncomfortable. I sensed frustration from her regarding my state of being and sleep issues.

Politics was a topic that we previously openly shared our thoughts and opinions, even if they differed, but something seemed to change. After my symptoms began, I found I could not handle our conversations. I was too overwhelmed. Kathy expressed frustration and anger with me at not being able to be the friend I was before which caused further anxiety on my part. Maybe it was hard for her to see me not being able to be myself. We decided to take a break from our walks "until I felt better." Eventually we parted ways.

***

I began avoiding almost all TV except baseball, especially news stations, sensationalism, talking heads, violence, and loud noises. Dan was mindful of my sensitivities.

"What do you want to watch?" Dan would ask.

"Watch whatever baseball game you want as long as the volume is low," I replied. "It's the only thing that is calming to me."

Loud music and lots of conversation was too much to bear. I became sensitive to light. I enjoyed going into our backyard in the summertime and laying in a lounge chair by the pool and looking at the mountains, but the sunlight was intolerable. I also lost the ability to read with cognition. That was difficult because reading was a hobby that was interesting and relaxing.

The overactivity of my nervous system was getting worse. Dizziness was a regular occurrence. At times I would collapse for no reason. Other times my legs would tremble, and I would grab onto something so I wouldn't fall to the floor.

Before bedtime I would run a warm bath to try to relax. When I got out, I left the water to cool so that I could return three to four times a night when I would awaken with zaps in my body.

***

As time wore on, my apathy increased. I gradually stopped doing my regular personal tasks such as putting on makeup and dressing professionally for my jobs. I continued reporting on Zoom but found it difficult with my confusion trying to organize exhibits and proofread. The coordinator for the company in which I worked was very understanding and assigned me the easiest jobs such as workers' compensation and personal injury as I requested. I was blessed to have someone like her who was willing to work with me.

I wanted to fill my time with the job I loved and that I had been confident in doing. I knew the excellence with which I had always performed was waning. As time went on, I lost more cognition and eventually the ability to retain words and phrases and, sadly, ceased working altogether.

Dan did most of the shopping and picking up dinner. I was not used to someone else taking care of what I felt were my duties.

I feel so useless not being as productive and high-functioning as usual. This is not me!

There was a very strange thing that I noticed within my brain months down the line. I had always been fastidious about buying everyday products before they ran out as I always tried to keep things stocked up. That thinking was gone.

The shampoo is running out, but I won't need any more anyway.

I ponder on the thought of people who give away their belongings before committing suicide.

Is this what the brain does to a person who is suicidal?

I question why psychiatrists and researchers have not studied the brains of those with suicidal tendencies. We all have heard about football players with post-concussions or veterans with PTSD who have committed suicide. I remember staying in our timeshare in Oceanside when NFL player Junior Seau took his life after having concussions. His home was a quarter mile down the strand from where we were and was decorated with balloons and flowers as mourners gathered around. PTSD, strokes, dementia, and other maladies of the brain are cellular and can be seen on a SPECT scan. The knowledge that Aviv Clinics do the proper testing and can heal brain damage should give hope to the many who are battling such an injury.

Chapter 4

My search for any medical intervention began within a few weeks after the day the symptoms started. I made a doctor's appointment with my primary care physician, Dr. Romero. She was a Venezuelan woman probably in her forties with whom I enjoyed a physician-patient relationship for about a year.

When I arrived at the center for my appointment, I donned the hospital mask handed out by an assistant at the entrance and had my temperature taken before being called into the examination room.

I reported my symptoms to Dr. Romero as we strived to communicate through the masks as well as her thick accent. She had no idea why I was having the issues I had, but she referred me to an ear, nose, and throat specialist for the tinnitus and prescribed Trazodone for the insomnia.

***

For the next week or so I took the Trazodone as instructed, but I still was not sleeping any longer than a few hours at a time.

This is so frustrating! I just want to sleep like I used to!

There is what is known as sleep anxiety that emerged which made things even worse. Worrying every night before I went to bed instead of relaxing the mind in order to shut down wasn't happening, even with using breathing and meditation techniques in which I had been proficient.

I craved that affinity for sleep that I had before all the symptoms began. I just wanted something that would put me out.

***

At my follow-up appointment with Dr. Romero, once again struggling to communicate through the masks and her accent, I reported how the Trazodone was not effective in helping me get a good night's sleep. To my surprise, she seemed exasperated with me as she had always been friendly and caring on our past visits.

She commented, "You are having hearing problems."

How dare you? It's the stupid mask and your thick accent!

At that point I knew she wasn't willing to fully care for what I was dealing with and instead projected her own issues onto me.

As luck would have it, I later made an appointment at the same medical center but with a different physician because Dr. Romero was unavailable the day I requested. Dr. Campos, who was a young, fit-looking gentleman with a USC lanyard who was very pleasant and showed interest in my symptoms on our first visit.

I asked him, "Do you think the COVID-19 vaccine could have caused this?"

He replied, "There's not enough that we know about it."

All the appointments I had with him he was very concerned about me but was dumbfounded. That first visit he ordered an array of blood tests, including thyroid tests.

***

As background, in 2012 my previous primary care physician noticed a lump on my throat and sent me to an endocrinologist who ordered a biopsy of the nodules on my thyroid. The test results came back "inconclusive" for thyroid cancer, but the endocrinologist recommended removal of my thyroid as a precaution. As it turned out, I had Hashimoto's Thyroiditis and not cancer. Had I known then what I know now after everything I have been through, I would not have had my thyroid removed. Thyroid cancer is slow-growing, and I feel the surgery was not necessary. I now have to be on medication for the rest of my life.

***

When the blood tests came back and Dr. Campos went over them with me on our second visit, the results were normal, except the thyroid level was low which meant I was in hyperthyroid mode. He decreased my Synthroid medication.

Maybe if I get my thyroid level to normal, it will take care of all my symptoms and get me back to normal.

I was intent on reading everything I could get my hands on regarding the thyroid and waited the six weeks for another blood test to see if the level was back in the normal range. Dr. Campos also referred me out to an endocrinologist.

***

I was also seeing a counselor to help sort out emotions from a year and a half of extended family issues and the seeming changes of the 25-year friendship. My mother passed away October of 2019 after her 12-year battle with Alzheimer's disease, so besides the pandemic fear that was put upon us, the protests and destruction of property we were witnessing on our television screens, and the political upheaval, I was distressed over decisions made by my father regarding the family trust and another personal issue. I was seeing a therapist by the name of Mary over Zoom.

At our first session after my symptoms began, she asked me if it could be because of thyroid imbalance which also made me focus more on that for the next few months. I also told her about how inconsistent the Trazodone was, but she convinced me to keep taking it.

I also explained to her that I was starting to become more and more hopeless.

***

At the visit with the ENT to which I was referred, she examined my ears and told me to stop drinking coffee and to have a hearing test.

A specialist telling me this? What a waste of time!

***

I got a phone call out of the blue from the son of a long-time friend who was an ENT at UCLA, and I explained my symptoms.

"It sounds like tinnitus."

I asked, "Could the COVID shot have caused it?"

He replied, "Not enough is known about it so I can't comment."

He continued to explain about tinnitus and the brain. I was very grateful that he took the time to call me and consult with me.

***

The appointment with the endocrinologist was set for a Thursday morning. This doctor was very young and soft-spoken. She seemed to be a fairly new practicing physician. Dan accompanied me as he was curious about my condition and wanted answers.

The thyroid levels were still in the hyperthyroid range.

"Doctor, would it be okay to go off the Synthroid to get the level down?" I asked.

She nodded and said, "Come back in two weeks."

I ceased taking the Synthroid medication.

Within a week of being off the Synthroid, I felt chest pressure and noticed my heart pounding very fast even if just walking to the bathroom.

What is happening? Am I having a heart attack?

It was early in the morning and Dan had gone to play softball, so I drove myself to the local medical center emergency room. Notably, there was no one else waiting in the lobby of the ER. I was admitted and given blood tests and Benadryl. The thyroid stimulating hormone (TSH) level came out in the very high range which meant I was very hypothyroid. The hospital staff questioned why a doctor would order me to cease taking Synthroid instead of lowering the dose since I had no thyroid. My systolic blood pressure reading was 157 from a usual low reading of 80 to 90.

Before being discharged from the ER, my endocrinologist was informed of the results, and I was given a starting dose of Synthroid and a scheduled appointment with her six weeks away. This was only one of two times I went to the ER thinking I was having a heart attack.

Chapter 5

In May Dan and I flew to Oahu, Hawaii, to visit our daughter and son-in-law who were stationed at the Marine base in Kailua. Jeff was a Chief Petty Officer working as air crew. Kelli was graduating with her MBA at Hawaii Pacific University, so we were going there to see her graduation ceremony. We were so proud of her. She completed her tour of four years in the Navy as a helicopter mechanic with a deployment to the Middle East. She then got her bachelor's degree in accounting at Jacksonville University, and now she was graduating with her MBA. She was also studying for the CPA examination.

I had a lot of trepidation about visiting Kelli and Jeff.

I'm nervous about visiting when I am like this. How am I going to sleep with the change of the time zone? I don't want Kelli and Jeff to know what's happening with me. No one understands what this feels like! Just act as normal as you can.

As I boarded the plane and sat in my seat, I made a quick phone call to my OBGYN who was also a friend to ask him about what could be causing my condition. I felt panicky and wanted answers to resolve my issues. We only had a few minutes to talk. I asked him if it could be menopause and wanted a quick fix. We weren't able to communicate well over the phone with the background noise, and we soon ended our conversation. It was very unfair of me to put that on him out of the blue.

After we landed at the Honolulu airport, we met Kelli outside of baggage claim and gave each other our usual hugs. On the way to her home, we stopped at Whole

Foods, and I once again picked up all the natural sleep aids I could find. I just did not like taking prescription sleeping pills. Kelli had known something was going on with me, but I think she thought I was just dealing with retirement. After we spent the rest of the day together and it was time for bed, the lack of drowsiness and tossing and turning was no different than any other night since all the symptoms began.

Kelli came into our room late that evening and said, "You haven't slept yet, Mom?"

"No," I replied.

"Just let it happen," she responded.

It was hard to explain to anyone how it felt It was like the sleep system in my brain was not working. I continued to toss and turn all night after having taken some of the sleep supplements which were not effective.

At the graduation I pushed through the ceremony trying to enjoy it the best that I could, but I was almost Zombie-like and still having the nerve sensations throughout my body.

That night, like every other night, was the same lack of sleep. I decided I would take a Xanax on the flight home and sleep but to no avail.

***

I was coming home to deal with the same symptoms. Yet they seemed to be getting worse as far as the brain fog and my mental and emotional state. I was beginning to feel suicidal but knew it was not something in which I would follow through. In my mind Bryce and Kelli were my reasons for living, and it was something I would not want to do to any of my loved ones, especially Dan. He had been understanding and frustrated for me about what was happening to me. I was so blessed to have a husband that would stick with me through everything that would happen in the next year and a half.

He always said, "We are together on this. I am with you."

Chapter 6

As the months wore on, I became more fearful. I had already developed sleep anxiety, and I was afraid that I would never be able to live with my distorted view of the world.

What kind of life will I have for the next 30-plus years? Am I going to be like this forever? How am I going to deal with the normal losses of life? How will I deal with losing Dan?

It was not the normal feeling of fear of a specific thought, but a generalized fear of everything. Even looking at a beautiful tree was frightening. It was like each next thing I put my attention to caused terror. I dealt with issues in life that were fearful, but I knew I was a strong person with the ability to overcome them. The fear of going out in public was increasing because of my deep sense of loss of control of everything I was and that others would notice. Going to places such as stores and restaurants I felt as if I were living in the twilight zone. The world in which I was living was distorted. It was bizarre. Yet I forced myself to go out as much as I could because I had learned not to give in to fear.

To try to describe the symptoms to anyone was incomprehensible. No one could understand. It wasn't like the flu or anything with which I could compare. Yet from the outside I looked normal. I think that's why most people just blew it off. There is no way anyone can even comprehend it. I felt very alone. The gaslighting became very callous. Not only did most physicians, therapists, and hospital staff disregard my symptoms and the cause, but, worse, my extended family wouldn't even consider it. A few friends were downright condescending. I was crazy, menopausal, still grieving Mom, having a nervous breakdown, or diagnosed with anxiety.

I would hear, "You need to take Paxil," "I think you should check yourself into a mental hospital," or "You're a liar."

***

As I have since learned from attending medical conferences, listening to frontline doctors, and being a member of React19, the gaslighting was a common occurrence that doctors and the general public went through with the COVID-19 vaccine. The propaganda machine was in high gear during this time pushing their "safe and effective" banner. The lack of trials and reporting of injuries were deliberately censored but are now emerging from the truthtellers who witnessed the lying firsthand. (Steibers, 2021).

Brooke Jackson was a regional director employed with Ventavia Research Group, a company that contracted with Pfizer to conduct quality control checks of the vaccine, witnessed "that the company falsified data, unblinded patients, employed inadequate trained vaccinators, and was slow to follow up on adverse events reported in Pfizer's phase III trial." "After repeatedly notifying Ventavia of these problems," she "emailed a complaint to the US Food and Drug Administration (FDA). Ventavia fired her later the same day." (BMJ, 2021)

On January 26, 2023, a U.S. judge blocked California Assembly Bill 2098, signed into law by Gov. Gavin Newsom, which sought to penalize doctors who spread "misinformation or disinformation" about Covid-19. Greg Dolin of the New Civil Liberties Alliance stated, "At no point has the State of California been able to articulate the line between permissible and impermissible speech." *(Reuters, Brendan Pierson, January 26, 2023.).*

Medical insurances and hospitals were given financial incentives to promote the vaccines. *(Providers.Anthem.com)*

A friend who worked as a nurse in Buffalo, New York, was only one medical worker who was fired for reporting COVID-19 vaccine injuries to the VAERS system as she was required to do.

***

As my feelings of fear progressed, one morning in June as I lay in bed after a night of partial sleep, I told Dan that I felt like I wanted to kill myself and that maybe I should go to the hospital. He suggested we call my therapist Mary. Mary advised me to go to the emergency room at a medical center that was highly reputable and was in the next county because she had confidence in their mental health treatment. It took us about 45 minutes to drive to the medical center.

I walked to the doors outside the emergency room and spoke with the intake person and told her that I was feeling suicidal. She took my information and guided us into the lobby to wait.

My name was called in a little over an hour, and I was taken into a back room as Dan followed, and the doctor came in to ask me questions. She was a large, attractive African American woman who listened intently and was compassionate to my plight. I explained to her my symptoms about my brain buzzing, the lack of sleep, and the other symptoms. She decided to send me for a CT scan of my brain at the imaging area of the hospital.

After I had the CT scan and the results came in, the same doctor came back to the same room where we had returned and told me everything looked normal.

I was then given a bed in the area of mental health patients where I and a few others were observed before a psychiatrist visited. I repeated my complaints to the psychiatrist and stressed the lack of sleep. I was given a larger dose of Prozac, 40 milligrams from 20 milligrams.

I had been prescribed the small amount of Prozac in my 30s for depression that ran in my genes while I was in group therapy for childhood issues. I found that the Prozac "cut the edge off" my more sensitive emotions and helped me to live more positively.

In the ER I was also prescribed Seroquel for sleep, which, as I later learned, is also an antipsychotic.

Did they think I was psychotic? Am I psychotic? Have I become crazy at 61, or have I been like this my whole life without realizing it?

This was a whole new area for me that was very scary. I always heard about the stories of older women in my grandmother's time who were committed to psychiatric hospitals when they hit menopause because they just went crazy.

Is this me? Does it really happen? Is this me?

My mother was very troubled her whole life and had a few breakdowns, one as a teenager and another when I was four and my sister was two. She received life-long therapy and heavy-duty medications which helped her through her days. Extended family members would express to me that I was becoming like my mother.

Am I all of a sudden at 61 becoming like Mom?

Although I loved my mother, we were as different as oil and water. It was a frightening thought for me, but if I could cope and it got me to just enjoy smelling the flowers and socializing, even for some moments, I was getting to the point where I would learn to accept it.

***

As Dan and I left the hospital, we discussed not telling Bryce or Kelli because we didn't want to worry them. We went home, and I intended on following hospital orders.

That evening, I took the Seroquel as prescribed and slept quite well. A downside to taking Seroquel for sleep is it takes a couple of hours for it to take effect.

The next morning, I was quite drowsy.

How am I going to be able to work while taking this medication?

I took a job that day and was able to get through it with little problem, at least that I could tell.

***

I continued on the Seroquel for a few weeks but got tired of feeling totally out of it during the day. I had always been sharp and active, but taking this medication I felt was turning me into a Zombie. I went back to the Trazodone and would add Xanax, Benadryl, or Tylenol PM so I could get some sleep, usually just three to six hours a night. As I have said, I did not like taking medications, but when prescribed, I had always adhered to the doctor's prescribed dosages, but now most of the prescribed dosages would not be enough to sleep. I came to a point where I realized I might have to resolve within my mind that this sleep issue may last a lifetime, so I better learn to cope with it.

Chapter 7

At my follow-up appointment with Mary, she strongly suggested that I get into a Cognitive Behavioral Therapy program through the same medical center I had just visited. I was willing to do anything to get better.

Whatever it takes to get better I will do. If I do have a different kind of depression and anxiety, I'll get therapy and take whatever medications I need to feel normal.

I took her advice and applied for the program and began within a few weeks. It was a five-week outpatient program for three to four hours a day with up to eight people. We also would see a psychiatrist for medications at least once a week.

***

Starting in my 20s, I spent about twenty years on and off in group therapy and some individual therapy for childhood issues. My therapist, Dr. Lorna Forbes, was a renowned psychiatrist who had been in the field for over forty years when I began seeing her. She was appointed by the courts as an expert witness in many cases, including O.J. Simpson's case regarding custody of his and Nicole's children. She also treated other famous people. She still practiced therapy as a psychiatrist which was how psychiatry was performed in earlier days. In the modern era, psychiatrists began only prescribing medications and psychologists, or marriage family therapists performed counseling.

I received a great education on people's psyches from Dr. Forbes. She would teach us a lot about the psychology behind one's behavior, even learning about Freud and contents of the DSM. Most of all, she helped me to understand my inner workings and the dysfunction within my family. I learned how to identify and process emotions and see things much clearer in order to live a prosperous and happy life. I feel very fortunate to have experienced therapy with her as I am able to read people's emotions and reactions very well.

***

From the beginning of the five-week cognitive behavior therapy (CBT), I found that I couldn't process what was asked of us patients. It was so basic to me, yet I couldn't grasp it. I had dealt with the issues that were being talked about years before.

Have I not totally dealt with my issues? Am I in denial?

I just didn't have the same intense emotions about things that others had. I had already come to terms with these things. My brain wasn't taking the information in like I knew it should. I kept thinking something would click, but it never did. I just couldn't feel emotionally except for desperation. I was numb.

I also met with the psychiatrist one to two times a week regarding medications. I told her about the lack of sleep and the nerve issues. She prescribed 1200 milligrams of Gabapentin which I took for two to three weeks and still was unable to sleep any longer than three to six hours and some nights not at all.

The last week I was in the program the psychiatrist

took me off the Gabapentin and prescribed me one milligram of Ativan. The Ativan helped me sleep better, but some nights I still couldn't sleep more than a few hours.

I don't want to become addicted to benzodiazepines, but if this is going to work, I guess I'll have to take it. I want to be able to know I am going to sleep and not be anxious about it.

***

After leaving the treatment center, I began seeing another counselor since Mary took on a professorship at the local university and had much less time to see patients. Katie was an attractive lady with long blonde hair who worked during the daytime at the same eminent medical center where I visited the ER and attended the CBT program, and she saw private patients in the evenings. We quickly developed an excellent therapist-patient relationship.

After about a half dozen sessions, she said, "This has to be biological. I've never heard of anyone suddenly developing a mental illness at your age, especially after a productive, healthy life."

What a relief to hear her say that! I know I don't have the answers on how to heal, but maybe there will be treatment in the future.

I felt comfortable because I wasn't being gaslit as was usually the case.

Chapter 8

The weekend after leaving the treatment program, using all the courage I could muster, Dan and I flew to Houston for our 37th wedding anniversary to visit Joel Osteen's church. I had recently begun listening to Joel as a way to find hope. My faith and prayers I kept close to my heart every minute of every day. The loneliness of feeling like no one could relate and with nothing to help heal me was unbearable.

God, please help me and give me the miracle of healing. I don't know how I can go on like this.

Most of my life I was an avid seeker of spirituality and philosophy. I read books and watched videos by Dr. Wayne Dyer, Rumi, Mark Nepo, and many others and studied Eastern religions at the local university. I spent a year in 2005 becoming a yoga instructor, so I was familiar with the Hindu and Buddhist philosophies. I had read books about living a life of uncertainty. It was a concept that I felt every day during this ordeal. In fact, it felt more like a black hole than anything else. I prayed for hours a day begging God to heal me. I wanted to die every day, but the phrase, "Don't give up!" was something that kept me going each minute of every day.

I also began journaling my prayers pleading to God to heal me. In my journal I wrote down the medications I had taken the night before and my symptoms throughout the day and would rate them from one to ten as the symptoms would change daily and sometimes hourly. I would spend hours re-reading my journal trying to figure out if there was anything I could identify that was a trigger for my symptoms.

I was blessed to have people who supported me. They were as dumbfounded as to the changes in me and felt frustrated and worried for me, but they were kind and gentle and would include me in their gatherings at a moment's notice depending on how I was feeling.

My dear friend Sandy prayed daily with me, and we read inspirational messages together. She told me to imagine a beautifully wrapped box with a new and wonderful life inside the box as my future.

Another friend Barb sent me inspirational videos and always included me in social events depending on how I was feeling.

One of my dearest friends, Devin, brought me little gifts of lavender and cards with written messages of hope.

Lori, a friend of 40 years, listened to my crying as I was curled up in a ball on the floor and gave me words of hope and prayer.

Conversations with my life-long friend Brenda who was a therapist gave me validation in her opinion of the cause of my condition being from the vaccine.

My friend Susie was upbeat with me and was always ready to lend an ear and reassure me. In fact, she accompanied me to a few of my doctors' appointments, even living two hours away.

My in-law Angie knew almost from the beginning that it was the COVID-19 vaccine that caused my plight. She was a pillar of strength and wanted me to come and stay with her at her place in Ft. Myers Beach, Florida, but I felt incapable due to the fears of my brain not being able to comprehend or organize enough to travel alone.

I was also asked to vacation with my good friend Jeanne at her condo in Maui, but, same situation, my mental inability to go anywhere plus my ineptness to pack and organize felt useless.

My aunt and uncle had a home in Lake Arrowhead that Dan and I would visit regularly. Lake Arrowhead is a beautiful, quaint mountain town in the San Bernardino mountains about an hour from Big Bear. It was a place where I felt safe to get away and sit outside watching the blue jays and woodpeckers, feeling the cool breeze, and just be. It helped just being in a calm place away from home.

My children were in the dark about what was happening and were frustrated about their feelings that they were losing their mother, but they were supportive. I did not want to put any burden on them or worry them. On the days that Bryce was working, he would stop by to see how I was. I was concerned about telling Kelli too much because she was already stressed studying for her CPA examination. She and Jeff were also going through IVF treatment, and I didn't want to cause any more stress. She didn't know the extent of my deterioration until much later.

Dan would play his usual senior softball three to five times during the week up until I could no longer be alone. When he was home, we would sit outside at the patio table under an umbrella by the pool for hours.

I would cry constantly, "When am I going to get better?" "Am I going to get better?"

My crying got worse and worse as time went on. I had never been a crier, but now my tears were like waterfalls of frustration at not being able to reach out and touch the beauty and enjoyment that I had always felt throughout my life.

I lost my emotional connection with people and with nature. I lost motivation to do anything but instead forced myself to do everything, including bathing and cooking.

Fake it till you make it!

I knew I had to function to avoid depression, although sadness, grief of the loss of myself, and depression was within me. I was scared to death that this was my life forever. Most things that used to bother me I never thought about anymore. The well-known saying "Don't sweat the small stuff" was reality in my life. It was crazy to me when I heard people complain about the littlest things. I couldn't grasp it.

I got a text from a former friend that said, "I cringe when you use the word 'chat.'"

Really? That bothers you? And I feel like I'm struggling every moment to survive.

I thank God for Dan. I don't know how he stayed with me and gave me his loving attention for such a long period of time and witnessed constant crying, my physical reactions to the frustration I was feeling, and basically the loss of his wife as he knew her.

Chapter 9

The month of September 2021 rolled around, and my sister Deanna planned a birthday party for our father one afternoon. It was a nice, warm day for celebrating his 85th birthday outside in his backyard. It was special for him since all his grandchildren except one, his two daughters, and his sister-in-law and brother-in-law were present.

Dan had plans to go to a softball tournament for five days, leaving directly from the party. I knew of the plans as we had previously discussed them and agreed to it. Softball tournaments were something Dan did three to four times a year with my blessing. It was a time I had usually looked forward to having some quiet time, and I was happy that he was so passionate about it.

This time was different though. I was afraid to be alone. I begged him not to go. At my father's birthday party, I began sobbing. I was deeply frightened. I continued crying and could not stop. Dan comforted me but left for his tournament anyway. I felt as if I were going crazy! My family tried to comfort me the best they could.

After leaving the party and going home, I lived every moment of that week putting one foot in front of the other, making contact with comforting friends and my therapist Katie, and made it through until he came home.

***

The cascade of tears became a common occurrence. I just couldn't help myself. Dan felt helpless but would sit with me and try to comfort me the best he could. Any kind of loud noise or outbursts from people or angry rhetoric would set my body feeling like it was on fire. Emotionally I was overwhelmed. I had to be especially careful with any kind of upset a few hours before bed or I would not sleep at all, even with medication.

***

The holidays of 2021 was a time of going through the motions. Christmastime was always the most special time of year for me which I attribute to my mother. As a child, in spite of our family living our lives walking on eggshells and under a dark cloud, my mother gave my sister and me the gift of the true meaning of Christmas along with festivities that usually came with the season.

I have fond memories of visiting nativity scenes, enjoying the Pomona Christmas parade, Christmas plays at Citrus College, light shows, visiting Santa at Buffum's department store in Pomona, midnight mass, caroling and more. We went to Olvera Street in Los Angeles for Las Posadas and the traditional breaking of the pinata.

My sister and I looked forward to the holiday season every year as an escape from the usual distress our mother was plagued with for the remainder of the year. Not to say that it was pleasant every day during the season because as the actual day neared, we knew our mom's demons would rear their ugly heads changing the day's mood from festive and joyful to walking on eggshells.

***

This year was very different for me. I had no feelings of joy in seeing the beautifully lit shopping centers nor Christmas music which usually stirred my heart and soul. Every year I decorated our home to look festive. Yet this season I had to force myself to bring our tree down from the attic and decorate it, at least minimally, just to keep the tradition. I even sent out a few Christmas cards and gifts from Amazon. But it was difficult. Emotionally I was sad because I questioned myself and whether I would ever feel the joy of Christmas again.

When my birthday rolled around at the end of January, I just wanted it to pass. I received lots of sweet text messages, for which I was very grateful for the love and intentions of friends and family, but the messages were overstimulating for me. With each text message I would feel what I could only describe as my nerves on fire. My body's reactions were becoming more and more bothersome as time went on.

Chapter 10

In February of 2022 I began seeing a naturopath in Pasadena, California. I had learned of Dr. Arredondo from a fellow retiree at a luncheon who claimed she was helped with insomnia and gastrointestinal issues. Dr. Arredondo's services were not covered by insurance, so I was prepared to spend a good chunk of money. At this point I would have spent anything to get better.

On our first visit, I told Dr. Arredondo my thoughts on the cause of my problems and also that I needed to get my thyroid levels stable. She was vaguely agreeable that the COVID-19 vaccine could be the cause but said she was focusing on healing rather than the cause. I was given an order for myriads of blood tests, including thyroid levels, and was told that with IV ozone treatments, I would heal within ten weeks.

Her expression to me was, "I'm going to get you back!"

I was onboard and had confidence in her. She also gave me some natural sleep supplements to try to taper off the Trazodone along with many other supplements.

During the time of being treated by Dr. Arredondo, I was prescribed various thyroid medications such as Synthroid, NP, and compounded thyroid medication along with a multitude of supplements and the IV treatments. The ozone treatments would calm the nerves for a couple of days after the treatment, but on the third day the pins and needles sensations would return.

Many times, when I was at the office, I would be in

tears asking Dr. Arredondo if I would ever be back to normal. In the beginning she would reassure me, but it was apparent from the response of her staff and her that I became very wearing on them with my crying and pleading to heal me.

About eight weeks into the treatments and $15,000 later, I was given another order for blood tests. My thyroid levels increased dramatically once again. This time the TSH level was 88! I was super hypothyroid.

Later when I returned to my PCP Dr. Campos and showed him the results of the high TSH level, he referred me to the head endocrinologist at another medical center.

"I've never seen thyroid levels fluctuate like this. I want you to see Dr. Gupta."

At my visit with Dr. Gupta, when explaining to him my thought that the cause of my condition was from the COVID-19 vaccine, he replied that he had at least ten patients who had thyroid issues like mine since having the vaccine but that there was nothing that could be done about it.

At least there's one doctor who will admit that the vaccine could be the cause!

***

Around this time, I received an email with an Epoch Times article on Brianne Dressen and the story of her COVID-19 vaccine injury. As I read through it, I was stunned to learn of her symptoms and how they mirrored mine: the nerves, sensitivity to light, sound, and touch, fast heart rate, insomnia, and more. She explained how she as a young mother had to close herself off in a dark room for days and how the touch of her babies was excruciating. I felt her pain.

Brianne was in the trials for Astra Zeneca where she was injured and asked Astra Zeneca for help. She and others who were also injured were referred to the National Institutes of Health where they began treatment, but soon the injured were turned away and were told they needed to find help elsewhere. There was no place for help. Compensation for treatment was nil since the Big Pharma companies were given immunity back in 1986 for any emergency-use vaccines thereafter. *(National Vaccine Injury Compensation Program, H.R. 5546 – 99th Congress, 1985-1986, 10/14/86.)*

Brianne and Dr. Joel Wallskog, a prominent orthopedic surgeon who was also injured by the COVID-19vaccine, started up a nonprofit organization called React19 to raise money to help others injured from the vaccine to receive treatment and support and to bring legislation for remuneration by the government and Big Pharma. By the time of this writing, React19 has grown into over 35,000-plus injured members, members of loved ones who have died suddenly from the vaccine, and non-injured volunteers helping the cause. For more information on React19, go to React19.org.

Reading Brianne's story confirmed why life had drastically changed for me. That was the point that I knew it was from the COVID-19 vaccine. Still, many do not believe that people have been injured by it and think that we are all just crazy. They do not want to believe the

physicians, attorneys, and other professionals that have published studies on the mRNA and nanoparticles within the shot that have caused the devastating injuries, but instead, in my opinion, have made it a political issue. It is difficult to get people to humble their ego for the truth when they need something to give them an identity, even if it is a lie. The amount of nerve damage, myocarditis, pericarditis, mental problems, autoimmune disorders, and gut issues that I have witnessed the injured endure, plus the deaths, one would think would bring about compassion from human beings, but it seems something is getting lost within our humanity. The newest study that has emerged has shown that cancers have multiplied and not just beginning with Stage 1 or Stage 2 as is usually the case, but Stage 4 cancers, especially after the boosters.
(https://www.frontiersin.org/journals/oncology/articles/ 10.3389/fonc.2023.1267904)

Chapter 11

In April 2022, our son Bryce married Shelby. They had met, gotten engaged, and married in less than a year. The major changes that were happening with him so quickly were very difficult for me, let alone the small everyday life changes.

The wedding was outside at a beautiful venue in the middle of orange groves. I went through the motions as I needed to be as the mother of the groom, but I couldn't be the social butterfly that I was used to being. A lot of the people at the wedding were police officers and police staff whom I knew and wanted to show my love of their presence, but I put on an act that I was okay. I avoided mingling because I couldn't be myself feeling joy for the newly wedded couple, and I didn't want to put a damper on the wedding. I found myself having to excuse myself a few times to be alone so I could cry due to my frustration of not feeling like myself on their big day.

***

One afternoon around May of 2022, Kelli called me to let me know she was pregnant. It was an exciting time for her and Jeff and everyone in our family, but, again, as much as I knew it was wonderful news, it caused my body to flare more than normal. I was frustrated and angry because I wanted to be able to enjoy this happy moment hearing about my first grandchild and to be there for Kelli, but I just didn't have the capacity to feel joy. It was all angst.

In the following days, I prayed daily to my grandson in Kelli's womb since he was the closest to God to ask Him to heal me so I could be the grandma to him that my grandmother was to me. I just wanted to be normal again.

***

In May of 2022, the housing prices were reaching their peak, and interest rates were climbing quickly. Dan was adamant about selling our home and moving to Florida. This was the dream we had been waiting for once hearing that Kelli and Jeff were being transferred back to Jacksonville. I couldn't get my mind to do anything, let alone sell our house and move across the country.

Dan said, "This is the opportunity to sell at the top of the market. We need to do it now before interest rates climb higher."

I replied, "This is just too much! If we sell, you need to take care of everything. I will try to do what I can, but you will need to work with me on how I'm feeling at the moment."

A few times there was a realtor who stopped by our home looking for business. She was a petite, cute woman in her late forties who was full of energy. When she was invited into our home to talk about the sale, I could barely stand to be around her. It wasn't her. She was dynamite and such a sweet lady, but her high energy caused me to be overstimulated. Dan was sold on her being our realtor as she had sold three other homes in our neighborhood.

We had a good friend we had used before as our realtor who was highly prestigious in the field and had been in the area for years whom I wanted to hire, but since I put it all in Dan's hands, he made the decision. I felt bad not using our friend, but, as it turned out, Antoinette did a fine job. We sold our home $35,000 over the asking price, and she took off a percent of her realtor fees.

***

Getting the word that our home had sold caused me to feel the intense electrical stimulation in my body, and I began having tremors and convulsions. In the mornings especially the tremors and convulsions would come on. They also reared themselves sporadically throughout the day.

Dan would have to be patient with me regarding signing papers and opening up bank accounts. If I was having an extra bad day, I would cancel any meetings we had regarding the sale of our home at the last minute.

As far as packing, I had picked up boxes from Lowe's with the intention of slowly packing the items we would be taking with us. The times when I was feeling up to it, I would pack some items, but I only packed about eight boxes total. We decided to have an estate sale of most of our furniture since moving everything across the country with the moving company's cost plus the fees the state of California charged would have been $30,000. We hired a company to hold the estate sale and paid to have a POD to store and move the items we were taking.

Part of the deal with Antoinette was she was to work with the estate sale company to remove anything that was left because I was not cleaning out anything, including paper chip bags. I just couldn't do it.

Chapter 12

In June we had planned on making a lifestyle visit to The Villages, Florida. I planned out our trip on the days and moments that I was able to force myself to talk to agents making reservations and other necessities for travel. I knew this is what we had wanted for a long time, but I couldn't get it in my head to actually make the major changes. I knew that if I didn't have the problems I was having that it would be an exciting time and I could more easily make the move.

Any changes, including the weather, the daily new regulations such as not being able to water our lawn, wearing masks, not wearing masks, driving to a new destination, packing boxes, were upsetting for me. Something in my brain was not working! I had always been an adventurous person, even traveling by myself at times, visiting museums, going to retreats, and hiking alone.

***

The day came to be shuttled to LAX for our venture to Florida. I took some Xanax to make it through the airport and get my seat on the plane. After we landed in Orlando around dusk, we picked up our baggage and ordered an Uber which took us to the office in The Villages to pick up the keys for the bungalow in which we would be staying.

By the time we reached the quaint, little home, it was dark. Dan pressed the button to open the garage door, and inside was a golf cart, as is typical in almost every home in The Villages. We entered the home and were pleasantly surprised by the clean, new open area of the kitchen and living room, two bedrooms, two bathrooms, and a little white fenced-in grassy yard.

After we unloaded our luggage, we decided to take a drive in the golf cart. As we were driving down the dark streets, we were hearing horns honking.

What's going on? Why are people honking?

We pulled over in a parking lot and read the instructions on the dash of the golf cart and learned that golf carts were limited to driving only on paths designated for them, not major highways that we were driving!

As we drove to find a golf cart path, Dan looked over to me and nervously said, "Don't go that way, there's a cop!"

We finally found a golf cart path and chalked up our first night at The Villages as a lesson learned: Read the instructions!

During the five days of our stay, we got lost so many times and had to make U-turns and figure our way around. I can laugh at it now, but at the time it was almost intolerable.

***

The first full day at The Villages I went to an appointment to see Dr. Villa, a lung specialist and primary care doctor, who I had the fortune of finding back in California through making phone calls to doctors who would treat my condition. I had no idea that she was treating many COVID-19 vaccine-injured and Long COVID patients.

Dr. Villa is a beautiful, petite woman from the Philippines. Dan and I felt comfortable from the first time we met her. After I relayed my symptoms to her, she immediately said she was sure it is from the vaccine and told us of about other patients' conditions that were similar.

She gave me an order for a variety of blood tests to take to California so my insurance would cover the cost. She was testing for COVID-19antibodies, cytokines, any autoimmune disorder, and the blood tests that are normally tested.

***

The next few days, we met up with our realtor Shane. Shane was a handsome young man who was more of a quiet type and yet so kind. He took us to different homes for sale. My mind was so distorted, I couldn't tell what I wanted or where I was. I lost the ability to have preferences in my likes or dislikes or feel my intuitions that I had all my life.

Within a couple of days, we made a decision on a turnkey home to buy in the village of Mallory. Mallory was an area that was highly sought after because it was the highest point in The Villages. People were attracted to it because of possible flooding during a hurricane. We wanted a turnkey home because I had little ability to furnish a home, let alone organize buying silverware, dishes, and whatnot.

We met Shane at the real estate office in Sumter Landing, one of the town squares in The Villages, where we signed papers. Again, I was just told where to sign without reading the documents or caring what I was signing.

After signing the documents, we went back to the home now in escrow just to look around the neighborhood and to get a closer look at our new home. As Dan was in the front yard, he met the neighbors across the street. Kim and Scott were a very friendly couple who were originally from North Carolina and who also had places in St. Petersburg and the Bahamas. Dan came back to our home and asked me to come over to meet Kim and Scott and told me Kim wanted to show me something.

We walked across the quaint-looking street and into our new neighbors' home where we met. Kim then showed me a brochure, her pre-assessment, and DNA test from the Aviv Clinic. She explained about Aviv and the treatment that she and Scott were going through.

Maybe this Aviv place will help me get better. I want to go there and investigate it.

The next day Dan and I walked into the Aviv Clinic in the Advanced Medical Center building on the opposite side of the Brownwood Hotel located in the center of The Villages. It was like no medical facility I had ever seen. As we walked into the lobby of Aviv, I felt as if I were in a futuristic place with white everywhere and a picture of a bright blue brain at the front desk. There was a huge screen that had a Power Point explaining the concept behind the clinic's treatment.

I was introduced to a client ambassador named Pete who was very welcoming and led us to a group of chairs and a small table to meet. I talked with Pete about what I had been going through and that I was sure it was from the COVID-19vaccine. Pete was very kind and empathetic to my plight. Throughout our conversation I was in tears. Pete excused himself to ask if a physician was available to talk with me.

Within a few minutes Pete returned with Dr. Mohammed Elamir, or Dr. Mo, and both sat down across from me. Dr. Mo was a very tall, handsome man who was a father of toddlers who grew up in New Jersey. He was a physician of internal medicine and was employed with Aviv Clinic.

I tearfully explained to Dr. Mo about my journey up to this point as he listened intently and explained that Aviv was treating people based on studies that were published on people who had continuing symptoms from the COVID virus but that he wasn't aware of studies for treatment from the COVID-19 vaccine. He did speak of one patient who came into the clinic in a wheelchair from long COVID and left walking. This all piqued my interest.

When we left the clinic, I began researching Aviv and its studies and You Tube videos of those who had been through the treatment. After I watched a You Tube video of Patrick Bol from the Netherlands who went through the treatment at Aviv for long COVID, it helped me to understand the philosophy and the science behind it.

I think this may be the place to heal!

Yet, of course, I still had PTSD from the gaslighting

I had from all the medical facilities I had been.

***

Aviv Clinic is the most advanced hyperbaric oxygen treatment center in the world. It began at the Sagol Center in Israel and has clinics in Dubai and The Villages, Florida.

The whole idea of the treatment is the HBOT combined with a concept that won the Nobel Prize in 2019 for HIF (Hypoxia Inducible Factor) which, after so many treatments, along with physical therapy, nutritional changes, and cognitive exercises, causes stem cells within the bones to proliferate to a degree that it heals damaged cells in the body and makes new cells. For the full study on post-Covid, visit https://www.nature.com/articles/s41598-022-15565-0.

Chapter 13

When Dan and I arrived at Orlando airport to return home, we checked in our luggage, went through the TSA line, and went to our gate. At the time of our departure, passengers began gathering around the entrance to board the plane. The weather was stormy that day. As luck would have it, the flight was delayed due to lightning.

Dan and I were in the middle of a big crowd of people hoping the delay would not be too long. Standing in the center of the crowd, I suddenly dropped to the floor and put my carry-on bag underneath my seat and pretended as if I were just resting. It felt almost unbearable as I looked up at the faces surrounding me as electric shocks were running throughout my body. We finally boarded the plane and were off back to California.

***

The first week we were back home, the tremors and convulsions felt out of control. One day during that week I drove to different mental health facilities to check into. Each one that I visited told me they couldn't help me.

One of the facilities was a lockdown. I parked my car in a random stall and walked up a step to the large metal door, looked into the small rectangular window of the door, and knocked a few times. A female employee opened the door.

"I need to check myself in," I told her.

She replied, "Just have a seat outside on the bench and someone will be with you."

As I was waiting on the bench, a police vehicle pulled up alongside the curb in front of me. There was a disheveled man in the backseat. The officer got out of the driver's side and stood outside the door waiting for service. As I looked back at the side window of the patrol car, the man had his face pressed against the window looking at me and making various gestures with his mouth and waving his head around as his tangled hair fell on and off his face.

This guy is either very mentally ill or on mega doses of drugs. Kinda' scary. But I've seen a lot of this before in court. Hope he doesn't try to break the window and escape.

A male employee came outside and sat down next to me and had me fill out a short form. I handed it back to him after I scribbled my information.

As he looked it over, he said, "You don't belong here."

"Okay. Thank you," I replied.

I got up from the bench feeling more hopeless, got back in the car, and drove home.

I continued doing what I could to live life, but I was desperate. I then began scouring the internet for ways to die. I had thought about trying to find bullets to Dan's gun to shoot myself but couldn't fathom something so violent.

A gun would be the fastest and easiest way, but it's too violent. I don't want Dan to have to see that. It would also hurt Dan's chances of selling the house.

I Googled medications and the dosages needed to cause death. I had some leftover oxycodone from my hip replacement in May of 2020. My mind was preparing to die.

I'll never be able to be the wife, mother, friend, and person I knew I was inside. I'll never be able to love my grandson like I want. I can't feel love or connection to anyone. I just feel trauma.

***

As Friday of the second week after we got home from Florida rolled around, Dan left early in the morning to get the car tuned up. As I awoke, I knew I was done. I lay in bed contemplating my near death. I looked out our sliding glass doors at my rose garden and apricot tree that Dan planted for me some years earlier. The bird bath and St. Francis statue added to the sanctuary I felt daily before that April day.

I got up out of bed to go to the medicine cabinet and pull out the prescriptions that would be the source of my death. I went back into my bed to lay down for a time as I watched the clock.

I need to do this before Dan gets home.

I arose once again and poured the pills into the glass next to my sink and went back to my bed to lay down again and pray.

The next time I got up, I went to the sink and poured water into the glass and stirred the contents with my finger and again went back to bed to lay down and pray.

Some minutes later I got up out of bed for the last time, went to the sink, picked up the glass, walked back to the bed, looked up, and then drank the mixture. I picked up my rosary as I lay down for what I expected to be my last few minutes on earth.

Dear God, you know the torture I have been going through. I know you understand why this life is no longer livable. Please wrap me in your arms and take me to You. Thank you for the life you have given me. Grandma, Great-Grandma, and Mom, I am ready to come be with you. Please take care of Dan, Bryce, Kelli, Jeff, and our grandbaby.

I then said my last Hail Mary with the rosary clutched in my hands and closed my eyes.

Chapter 14

As Dan was in the middle of paperwork at the dealership selling the Nissan Rogue, he received a call from Kelli.

"Dad, Mom isn't answering her phone. I've called her and text her all morning."

"Let me try to get ahold of her," Dan said.

Dan called my phone number at least three times and got no answer. After calling and text messaging a few more times, worry began to permeate his thinking.

Concerned, Dan relayed to the finance manager, "I've got a situation at home I need to take care of. Would you hold the rest of the paperwork until I return?"

"Sure. No problem. I trust you," he replied.

Dan quickly walked to his car and began to drive home.

On the way home, Dan called his best friend Pablo.

"Hey, Pablo, I've been trying to reach Lynette, but she hasn't been answering my calls or texts. I can see on Life360 that her phone has been home all morning. Would you go check on her? The sliding glass door to our bedroom is open," Dan told him.

"Sure. I'll go right over," said Pablo.

Pablo was a tall, balding man with a zest for life.

He was a retired AP Spanish teacher at the high school, hence Pablo versus Paul. We met Pablo and his wife Vicki when our boys were in Little League. Vicki was also a teacher at the high school. They were beloved by everyone in the community.

***

Pablo arrived at our home about two miles from where he lived. He noticed the gardeners just leaving. Receiving no answer after knocking on the front door and ringing the doorbell, he walked into the backyard and went to our bedroom. Pablo opened the screen and moved the shades out of the way, and he noticed me lying in bed. As he got closer, he could see that I looked like I was sleeping with my left arm hanging out from the bed with the rosary on the floor. He could see my chest was rising and falling. He nudged my shoulders trying to wake me.

"Lynette, Lynette, wake up, wake up!"

Hearing soft moaning noises but unable to wake me up, Pablo called Dan.

"Hey, Dan, she's laying here in bed. I tried to wake her up, but she wouldn't awaken. She is breathing though."

Dan's heart dropped. "Call 911 because I'm in traffic."

Pablo did as Dan asked.

***

Dan finally arrived home after what seemed like an eternity. Seeing the emergency vehicles in front of the driveway, he parked in front of the neighbor's home and hurriedly got out of his car. The front doors were open. As he entered the house and proceeded to the bedroom, his first look was the paramedics hooking me up to an IV and taking vitals.

A paramedic approached Dan. "Do you know if she's been taking any medications?"

"She's been taking medications for not being able to sleep," replied Dan. "Maybe she accidentally took too many."

The two police officers recognized Dan as their colleague Bryce's father and greeted him.

The paramedics went out to their emergency vehicle, pulled out the gurney, and rolled it into the bedroom.
They proceeded to lift my limp body onto it. I was then transported to the local community hospital and admitted into the emergency room.

***

As Dan drove to the hospital, he called Bryce to let him know about the situation. Bryce and Shelby were on their way to celebrate Shelby's birthday.

Bryce said, "We're only 20 minutes away. We will be right over."

Then Dan called Kelli.

"Mom was unconscious, but we don't know what happened. It looks like she may have taken too many pills. We don't know if it's accidental or not."

"Oh, my God, Dad! Keep calling me to let me know how she is. I'm going to make flight plans to come there," replied Kelli.

Next Dan called Deanna, my sister, and explained the situation.

"Oh, gosh, Dan! I'm leaving my house now. I'll call my dad," Deanna responded.

Dan arrived in his SUV soon thereafter and went to the admitting window.

"My wife just got brought in here. Her name is Lynette Milakovich. I'd like to go see her."

The kind-looking admitting clerk responded, "Wait in a seat out in the waiting area and you will be called in."

Dan found a chair within the half-filled room and sat down. He was in shock. He did not want to believe it was intentional. His wife had never in all the years he knew her would try to kill herself. She just wasn't that way. All Dan could do was hope and pray that I would survive physically and mentally.

***

A female voice from the entrance to the emergency room could be heard. "Dan Milakovich."

Dan stood up and quickly walked into the ER doors following the nurse to where I lay unconscious. He noticed the monitors and IV hooked up to me.

The nurse looked at Dan and said, "She's stable. She will eventually wake up."

Dan asked the nurse, "Will you have to pump her stomach?"

"No. She'll be okay," the nurse replied with assurance.

Dan sat down in a chair next to my hospital bed as I lay unconscious.

***

My father and sister Deanna arrived and asked the admittance staff if they could see me. They were told only two people were allowed in the room at a time. The staff then conveyed the message to Dan that they were in the waiting room. Shortly thereafter Dan came out of the emergency room to the lobby.

"How is she?" asked Deanna.

"She's unconscious but stable. They are just waiting for her to wake up," replied Dan. "Why don't you both go in to see her."

My dad and Deanna walked inside the double doors to my bed. My dad was hurting seeing his oldest daughter in such a condition. He proceeded to rub my forehead.

Deanna knew that I had done this on purpose. She was someone I cried to on a regular basis and had said many times, "I'm scared. I'm afraid I'm going to kill myself."

As Deanna held my hand, she softly said, "Lynette, you're going to be okay. I love you."

As a nurse came over to check the monitor, Deanna asked her, "Why isn't she being given charcoal, or her stomach being pumped?"

"We don't do that at this hospital. We also don't know what she took, so we don't know what may be contraindicated," said the nurse.

Deanna and Dan stayed with me almost the whole time until others wanted to come in. They watched and waited for any sign of my awakening. My body exhibited convulsions throughout the time I was unconscious. There were moments when I would suddenly come to, mumble a few words, and fall back asleep.

As time went on, my mumblings would become more coherent.

When Dan saw that I seemed awake, he asked, "Why did you do it, Lynette?

"Because I don't want to be like my mom," I replied.

Then I closed my eyes.

***

Bryce and Shelby arrived and came into where I was as the others left. Shelby was a nurse and was able to see that I was stable. Bryce came over to my skinny body and pale face and started crying as I would tremble with convulsions.

I love you, Mom," Bryce said tearfully.

During this time there was a lot of discussion amongst Dan, Bryce, and Deanna with Kelli over speakerphone about what needed to be done with me.

Dan said, "I want her to come home."

"But, Dad, she needs help! It's not going to be any good bringing her home. The same thing will happen again," Kelli responded as Deanna agreed.

Bryce chimed in, "She needs to go into a drug rehab. I've already found one."

"She doesn't belong in a drug rehab!" Kelli exclaimed.

The bantering back and forth went on for a while until Kelli said, "Wait until I get there, and we can talk about it."

As Bryce and Shelby could see that I was stable and going to be okay, they left for their weekend to San Diego.

***

When awaking some time later, I spoke the words, "I talked to David. He said it's not my time."

David was Dan's oldest son from his first marriage. He was a good-looking young man who came to live with us at the age of 15 after his mother passed away. David was a sensitive person with a loving heart but was troubled. He began doing drugs and who knows what else when he was living in Northern California with his mother and older sister. When he came to live with us, problems started with his doing drugs and breaking into cars. He wound up in Juvenile Hall for a year. Eventually he wound up in state prison a few times with two strikes on his record for robberies.

When David was paroled, he became certified as a counselor for parolees and devoted himself to Christianity. He was clean and sober for about nine years and helped dozens of parolees and drug addicts become sober. Bryce and David became very close as Bryce would refer drug addicts to David to be helped.

The evening of January 8, 2018, we received a phone call from his roommates that they found David unconscious on the floor in his bedroom. Paramedics responded, and David was transported to St. Mary's Hospital in Apple Valley, California. We called the hospital and asked to speak with the doctor who was caring for David.

The doctor hesitantly said, "I'm sorry but David is deceased."

David was 43 years of age. We thought he died of a heart attack as he was heavy, didn't eat well, and lived an unhealthful life. The autopsy results came ten months later in October that David died of a methamphetamine overdose.

The psychiatrist came to speak with me when I was coherent and asked if what I did was willful. For a while I was denying that it was on purpose, but eventually I told her that it was purposeful.

"I don't want to live," I said.

The psychiatrist then spoke with Dan. "She's going to be on a hold for 72 hours. We are waiting for a bed to open up at a psychiatric facility, and then she will be transported."

As evening rolled around, Deanna lay next to me in bed all night as everyone else went home to get some rest.

The next morning as breakfast was brought in, I opened my eyes and told Deanna I didn't like the food they brought and that I wanted some fruit, something I was not aware of saying. Deanna needed a few things at the store, so when Dan arrived, she left for the store.

The nurse came in to speak with Dan. "A bed became available in Chino. AMR is on its way to transport her."

When Deanna returned with the fruit, the ambulance attendants were placing me on the gurney to be transported to the psych ward.

Chapter 15

My first awareness since saying my good-byes to the world was waking up in a twin bed the morning after arriving at the hospital in Chino. As I looked to my right, I saw a slight, blonde woman probably about 65 to 70 years of age asleep in the other twin bed. The room was bare of furniture or pictures.

Well, I didn't die. I deserve to be here for what I did. I wonder what it's like to be in a place like this.

Getting up to go to the bathroom, there was nothing but a sink, shower with no curtain or rod, and a toilet.

As I came back in the room, my roommate was awake.

"Hi! I guess you're my roommate!" the woman said.

"Hi. Nice to meet you. What is your name?" I asked.

"I'm Nancy. Let's go get our medication."

Nancy and I walked out of our room after dressing in our own clothes that were brought in for us and went to the nurses' station. We waited in line for our medications to be distributed.

This reminds me of "One Flew Over the Cuckoo's Nest." "Medication time!" I wonder if they know what I'm taking. Maybe Dan gave them the list of medications that I had written down at home.

As I got to the front of the line, a heavyset nurse asked my name and opened her notebook. She asked me what I was taking and then placed them into a little cup and also gave me a cup of water.

I then went into a large room where all the patients gathered. Soon breakfast was served.

Great! Cold scrambled eggs and toast and orange juice. The coffee smells good, but it will fire up my nerves. Just accept it! You did this to yourself!

Not having my usual nutritional meal of yogurt and fruit with some oats and herbal tea was something I had to go without.

The day was spent sitting around in the day room with the tv on. There were cigarette breaks for the smokers to go outside to a cemented area with tables and umbrellas, so I would go out with them to get a change of scenery.

***

There were two phones that were available near the nurses' station where I made phone calls throughout my time at the facility to speak with Dan, Bryce, Kelli, and other family members and friends.

"I am so sorry for what I did," as I cried to each person. "I didn't want to hurt you, but I couldn't stand what's been happening to me! I really thought I wouldn't be here."

Most of the responses were supportive and loving. Dan, of course, was torn up.

"I thought I lost my wife!"

There were still times where I lost connection with reality like when I called my dear friend Sandy.

"Hi Sandy! Would you bring me a blow dryer?"

Of course, patients were not allowed any electrical items. That call obviously was a time where I lost moments of awareness while being awake.

When I went to shower, I first had to go to a room with shelves that had sample shampoos and soap in little baggies and towels.

***

The three days I spent in Chino, I told myself, was a way I could see what the inside of a psych ward is like.

Gosh, this is so ironic. In court we sent people here, and now I'm here. I am the perfect example to show that any one of us could end up here. I get to witness what it is like to be in a place like this.

There was a very tall gentleman probably in his 20s or 30s who was very flamboyant. He wore bright green and purple clothes and strutted around making friends showing his warm personality in his higher pitched voice. He was an interesting character.

I befriended a young African American boy who I intuited needed someone to talk with. I felt as if he needed a mother figure. He was a sweet, respectable young man and seemed to feel comfortable with me.

I witnessed a few very sad incidents with a young blonde girl who I learned had been badly abused her whole life. She would hang onto the railing in the hallway and cry and scream inconsolably. I felt terrible for her. I just wanted to hug her. It just made me realize how traumatic it is for people who are dealing with the aftermath of abuse or mental illness.

A young Hispanic boy who came in the day before I would be discharged, I could tell was very uncomfortable. He reminded me of the young OVS gang members that we dealt with in court. As angry as it made me with some of the crimes the gang members committed, I felt bad for some of the young ones because that was all they knew having grown up in gang families. I tried to talk with him a few times as a mother figure, but it was difficult. Eventually he seemed to gain some trust and I think felt some comfort. At least I hope so.

***

The day of discharge came. As I was behind the nurses' station trying to help the attendant gather my clothes that were being held behind the desk, she became frazzled and got snappy with me and others.

"Keep your hands off the counter!" she yelled.

The patient with the flamboyance screamed back at her, "I'm supposed to be out of here now! I'm calling my lawyer!"

I gathered my clothes and discharge paperwork and was released.

***

As I went out the double doors to the outside, Bryce was standing about six feet from me. I quickly walked to him, and we hugged as I bawled.

"I'm so sorry, honey."

"It's okay, Mom. We're going to take you home."

I then saw Kelli and Dan and Deanna standing outside the RAV4 waiting for me.

We all drove straight home.

Chapter 16

Kelli, Bryce, and Deanna all agreed I needed mental health intervention. My guilt made me willing to do whatever they said. They also wanted me to stop taking all hormone and sleep medications. I ate cannabis edibles that week that helped me sleep.

Kelli researched and found a mental health treatment program in Costa Mesa. She was on the phone with the coordinator to get me admitted. They required all the hospital records. Kelli had the Chino records sent to the center, and we drove to the local hospital to pick up those records and faxed them over.

Kelli drove me to the office of Dr. Campos, my primary care doctor, in order to fill out an authorization form for her to be able to speak with him on my behalf. I also filled out a Power of Attorney leaving Kelli in charge of all decision-making of my medical issues and the ability to communicate for me. I was signing my life away to her.

It was the week before the July 4th holiday at home since I couldn't get admitted into the facility until July 6th. The POD to pack all our belongings to move to Florida was in our driveway and boxes were everywhere. I could barely stand the chaos.

"I can't handle this!" as I quickly paced throughout the house. "I don't want to leave my house!" or, "No! I want to take that with us!"

Dan and I argued over the dining room set.

"But I love the dining room set! I want to take it!" I cried.

"It's too big, Lynette! We will have to pay for another POD! We will get all new furniture in Florida," Dan assured me.

There were a few breakdowns during that week. I cried the majority of the time. I felt as if I couldn't stop crying. The convulsions became more intense and constant. Dan, Bryce, and Kelli were careful not to pack in front of me because it would set my nervous system off.

It will be better to be away at the treatment facility so they can pack without me here. I just can't deal with it.

***

Independence Day we celebrated in Lake Arrowhead on Saturday, July 3rd. Dan, Kelli, and I went to my aunt and uncle's place for the night. That Saturday early evening we took their boat out on the lake to watch the fireworks. Thankfully, my body happened to be in a calmer state, so it made for a more comfortable time.

Chapter 17

July 6th rolled around and Dan, Kelli, and I drove to the treatment center. Kelli had packed most of my items for me. She also recorded her voice along with Dan's and Bryce's on an iPod giving me hope while I was away. It was supposed to be a six-week stretch with the idea that I would get medications straightened out and some intense therapy, still thinking that might be the key to getting better.

I'm sure this is all caused from the vaccine, but if medications and therapy will help this time, I'll do whatever I need to do to get better. I owe it to Bryce and Kelli for what I did to do what they think I need.

We drove towards the Southern California beaches and into a residential neighborhood in Costa Mesa. We parked the car along the curb in front of the house where I would be staying. It was all enclosed by a dark blue wooden fence. Kelli called the center's number as we approached the gate. A few moments later a young dark-haired lady approached and opened the gate. She was very kind and welcoming and explained that Dan and Kelli were not allowed into the facility.

Okay, this is the time to go and leave my family. Off into never-never land again! I'm not ready for this! Why can't they come in with me! I don't want to be alone!

I bawled my eyes out as they gave me hugs and said their goodbyes.

"I love you, Mom."

"I love you, honey."

"I love you, too."

The attendant took my suitcase as I carried my pillow and a bag into the house. She guided me to my room. It was nicely decorated with two twin beds. I noticed another set of luggage and a few clothes lying on the bed and a book on the dresser.

I must have a roommate.

After I left my gear in the bedroom, the attendant took me around the house into the kitchen and showed me where everything was and the schedule for food and groceries. She then introduced me to two young ladies who were also staying at the facility.

I looked around the house and then headed up the stairs to the office where the young attendant sat behind the desk. I sat down in front of the desk.

"Am I going to get better?" I asked.

"We are going to help you. You will see a psychiatrist on Zoom, and he will prescribe medication and there will be private and group therapy," she responded.

"Thank you," I said. As much as I wanted to stay there for more reassurance, I got up from the chair and walked down the stairs.

There were large sliding glass doors that I walked through to the backyard where one of the young girls was sitting. She was a pretty blonde gal around 25 years of age who didn't say anything as I sat down next to her.

"Will I get better?" I asked.

She scantily replied, "I don't know."

I know I am bothering everyone asking the same question over and over, but I want to know I am going to get better.

I did notice some months before this of my having to have things repeated over and over by everyone I spoke with. It wasn't that I necessarily forgot, but it was that I needed reassurance constantly.

***

Dan, Kelli, and Bryce spent their time packing the POD with photos, clothes, and minimal items to move to Florida with the plan that all other items would be sold at the estate sale. As Kelli went through my drawers, she was shocked.

"My mom's lingerie drawers are a mess! She always kept them neat and orderly!" she said in a phone call to her mother-in-law Angie.

The packing up of our Upland home went on for a few days, and then Kelli headed home to Kailua. The POD was loaded on the truck and headed off to Florida. Dan left our home of 32 years to the Airbnb in Lake Arrowhead that my aunt and uncle so kindly rented to us.

***

Meanwhile back at the treatment center, I was interviewed for hours by a woman who I later found out was an intern, not the certified therapist that the law required. She was a meek lady whose insecurity was blatantly apparent.

"Have you ever – have you – have you ever – do you have –"

Come on, ask the question! She is so inept! I should be giving her therapy! And this is supposed to be a highly ranked facility?

As advertised, there was also supposed to be a nurse on duty 24 hours a day. There was no nurse ever on the property, only minimum wage workers babysitting us.

The second morning that I awoke, I decided I had had enough again. My roommate had already gotten up and left our room. I took the sheet off my bed and stuffed it under my sweatshirt so as to avoid the cameras in the hallway from seeing it.

I walked through the brown wooden bathroom door and shut it behind me. I walked into the shower and tied the sheet into a knot and hung it over the shower head. As I got on my knees, I put my head through the hole of the sheet and laid my neck in it. As the heaviness of my body went forward, I could feel the air being cut off as the sheet pressed against my throat. Seconds went by as I held my ground.

I'm done! Life is torture!

As I began feeling more light-headed, something came over me. It was as if I could hear Kelli speaking to me.

"Mom, stay alive for me! You are going to get better!"

I suddenly stopped myself and made the decision that I was going to push forward. I pulled my head out of the sheet, untied the knot, and once again stuffed the sheet under my sweatshirt. I walked out of the bathroom and back into my room and placed the sheet back on the bed. I then proceeded out of my room to the kitchen to fix some breakfast.

In the next couple of days we took a few trips in the van to the gym and to AA meetings.

Do I really need to be here at an AA meeting? I feel so out of place. But so sad some of these stories.

One morning we went to a park and took part in an American Indian ceremony. As we were leaving the park, I walked up to one of the attendants from the facility whom I felt support and told her I was having the same suicidal feelings.

The next morning a young woman who was an administrator came to the home and took me outside.

"We are sending you to a psychiatric hospital in Long Beach," she said.

"But I'm good here! Pleeez let me stay!"

"No. They will be able to get your medications squared away," she replied.

"But I promise I'll be okay. Pleeez!" I cried to her.

"No. You need to get your things together. The Uber is on its way."

I went back to my room and packed my suitcase and waited for the Uber driver. Once he arrived, he took my suitcase to load into the Prius as I followed him. I got into the back seat and looked out the window and saw the tall female patient with brunette hair. She looked straight at me with obvious worry and gave me a sweet wave as we drove off to the psych hospital.

Chapter 18

The Uber driver pulled into a parking lot next to a tall glass building that looked more like an office complex than a psyche ward. As I got out of the backseat, the driver already had the trunk popped open retrieving my suitcase. We walked into automatic sliding doors to the elevators. As the elevator doors opened, the driver motioned me in as he followed and pushed the button to the floor we would soon to be arriving. When we arrived, we both walked out, and I followed him to the suite door of the place I would be staying for four nights.

Walking into the small lobby, there were glass windows with an office full of staff. Behind them was a glass partition where I could see patients of all kinds of ages and races wandering, sitting on couches, and a couple playing ping-pong. One blonde lady around 50 years of age I could see as she was yelling at someone.

Well, here I go again. I don't want to be here!

As the Uber driver exited, the lady at the front desk greeted me.

"Hello. My name is Belinda. Here is some paperwork for you to fill out."

"I really don't belong here!" I replied.

"Well, this is voluntary. You don't have to stay," she said.

I began crying.

What am I going to do? I'm afraid to go home because I'm scared I'll try to kill myself again!

Another lady walked into the lobby and sat down next to me.

"Hi. My name is Desiree. I am here to help you. You don't have to stay if you don't want to."

"I'm just afraid to go home!" I cried.

"We can help you here. You will only be here to get your medications adjusted and get you stable," she explained.

I cried incessantly.

And I finally relented, "Okay. I'll go."

A dark, handsome man about 30 years of age came into the lobby and led me into the next room and asked me to sit in a chair. It was a small, brightly lit room with some countertops and a telephone.

As I sat there, he opened my suitcase and began going through each piece of clothing that I had.

"What are you doing? Why are you going through my stuff?" asking in a distressed manner.

"You are only allowed certain items here," he quietly replied.

"But why?" I asked.

He kindly replied, "It's for your protection. I'm going to need to take your necklace, too."

"No! You can't take that! It's a pendant from my soon-to-be grandbaby! I need that!"

"I'm sorry," he replied. "Hold on. I'll be right back."

He is being very kind. I can tell he feels bad for me.

A few minutes went by, and he walked back into the room.

"Okay. You can keep the necklace," he assured me.

"Thank you," I said.

After he went through my things, he walked me to the room I would be sharing with a young gal around 25 years of age. The room had two twin beds with a blanket and a large milk crate next to each bed. I unpacked my things and looked out the large window. I could see the city full of buildings within the smog-filled air. As I sat down on the bed, I noticed a tv hanging on the wall.

Well, that's a nice addition. I could watch baseball or Jeopardy.

I went out into the day area where everyone was sitting on the couch or at the tables where there were crafts. I introduced myself to the other patients trying to pass the time.

A lot of the patients I later found out would check themselves into hospitals like this so they could get their Adderall or other drugs. The staff were onto their manipulations, so arguments were a regular event.

***

The second day I had an appointment with the psychiatrist. Dr. Smith had been in the business for thirty years. He reminded me of a bookworm type of man but more friendly. As we sat at a round table, he pulled out a report on me.

"I see you are crying a lot. I find you have bipolar disorder, and I am going to order Depakote along with Seroquel for you," he said matter-of-factly.

"Okay," I replied.

I guess I am bipolar at 62 years old. Hopefully, the medication will straighten me out.

Our meeting lasted about five minutes and off I went back to my room.

***

The days were filled with meals being brought by on a cart where we would eat in our rooms because of L.A. County's order on COVID. At least we weren't wearing masks … yet. There were set times for medications. We did arts and crafts, played games with the staff, watched tv in the day room or our private rooms.

There was also available a phone for anyone to use at any time, so I spent time calling friends and family.

"I know this is from the vaccine," I told one family member. "I have experienced depression and some anxiety before, and this is not it. This is totally different."

She replied, "No, it's not," which was the typical response I would get from extended family members.

This is pissing me off! How can anyone judge me like this! They have no idea what this feels like! And all of a sudden, I'm bipolar and in a loony bin?

During each day all patients were taken outside into the parking lot for a smoke break. I would take walks around the parking lot, and sometimes others would join me.

Most of the patients at the hospital were friendly and didn't exhibit the mental issues they had. I was asked to lead a yoga class, so I tried to put together a few poses for those who were interested. It turned out to be a pleasant time.

Sleeping at the facility was difficult, not only because of the sleep issues I was having even with medication, but also the traffic from outside could be heard. I would wake up many times during the night from screeching tires or honking horns.

***

As the third day rolled around, a staff member came to my room and sat on the bed next to me.

"The residential treatment center that you came from won't take you back. There's a case of COVID. So, I found another place in Thousand Oaks," she told me.

"Oh, my gosh! Why? Well, okay, that's what I'll do," I responded.

The next morning, I packed my clothing and other personal items and waited with another gal to be picked up. Soon we were escorted down the elevators and into the parking lot where a black Cadillac Escalade was waiting for us. We looked at each other like "Wow!" as the dark curly-haired driver opened the doors for us, grabbed our luggage to put in the back, and drove off to our next stop.

Chapter 19

The black Escalade pulled up in front of a one-story home in an upscale neighborhood filled with oak trees.

"Corinne, this is where you will be staying," said the driver.

Corinne exited the SUV as the driver unloaded her bags, and they walked up the walkway to the house.

The driver quickly got back in the Escalade and drove just a few blocks away to a two-story home in which I would be staying. I unbuckled my seatbelt and stepped down onto the driveway and began walking up the walkway as I was met by a middle-aged thin brunette lady.

"Hi, my name is Denise. I'm one of the nurses here," she said.

"Will I get better?" I asked.

She responded, "Yes. We will do everything we can to help you."

As we walked into the foyer, I noticed the modern décor with positive wording on signs and pillows.

How nice! I only wish I could feel the meaning of those quotes inside me.

Denise led me into the central room where the office was. I was met by a young lady named Alicia who asked me to sit on a chair next to the desk in which she sat.

I went through an interview process regarding my medications as she brought out a rectangular plastic container in which to place them.

Alicia then proceeded to take me into the kitchen where I met the other patients. A few were eating while a couple others were cleaning up.

"Hi ladies, this is Lynette. This is Teri, Sam, Margie, Christy, and Brenda," Alicia said in an informal manner.

The responses were short and nonchalant.

Alicia then guided me into the laundry room and explained the layout of the house, the schedule, chores, and outings. Past the laundry room was a door that led into a converted garage where group therapy was held. There were seven comfortable-looking chairs with pillows plus a TV on the wall.

Alicia and I then returned back through the kitchen and up the tile stairway with black wrought iron rails to a large bedroom where I would be staying.

"You will be sharing this room with Margie. Here's your bed," Alicia said.

"Thank you," I replied.

Alicia continued, "I'll let you be here to rest. If you are hungry, there's dinner downstairs in the kitchen," she kindly said.

"Okay. Thank you."

The room had two twin beds with large windows where you could see oak trees and pine trees as the scenery outside. I sat down on my bed and noticed a journal and a pen next to it on the end table.

Oh, good, I'll be able to journal my experiences in this whole new place of uncertainty.

After resting for a few minutes, I went downstairs to the kitchen and dished up some spaghetti and salad and sat at the long wooden table with the other ladies as they conversed with each other. By this time, I had pretty much given up any concern about my stricter healthy eating. After all, the places I had been to weren't too concerned about healthy eating. After finishing my dinner, I cleaned up my dishes and sat back down at the table with the others. I began to cry.

"Am I going to get better?

Margie responded, "Do what you need to do here, and you will get better."

A couple of the other women piped in.

"Yes. You just need to go through therapy, and it's an everyday process."

As I cried, I told them, "I've had a lot of therapy. I've never felt before what I feel now. I know it's from the vaccine."

As a few gave me looks like I was crazy for even thinking that Brenda quickly spoke up. "It's not from the vaccine. You need to get ahold of yourself."

The next day I was introduced to my therapist. Dr. Brown was a large woman who usually wore all black including a black mask with her name in bright white with "BA, MA, PhD" following for all the world to see. Our first session was a pleasant one. I explained to her about the therapy I had in the past and the dysfunction within my family.

When I told her I felt as if what I was dealing with was from the COVID-19vaccine, Dr. Brown replied, "Oh, sure, it may very well be, but you are going to have to learn to deal with it."

At least someone here acknowledges what I know inside. But how can I deal with this for the rest of my life? I've tried to kill myself once, and I don't know of anything that will change that, unless there's a drug I haven't tried yet. Maybe in time. I'm not going to give up at this point for everything my family has been through.

***

For the first two weeks of the 30- to 90-day stay, I was not allowed any phone calls or visits. We pretty much spent our time coloring rocks, doing a type of needlepoint with tiny stones, going to therapy, and meeting with a psychiatrist once a week and private therapy two times a week, although private therapy with Dr. Brown was cancelled on me at least three times. I could only guess why.

We also had outings to a horse farm where we brushed and walked the horses and to another farm with llamas and goats. We attended a yoga class once a week.

I could tell I was wearing on the ladies. They were frustrated with my constant crying. Soon the bullying began, particularly from Teri. She was experiencing PTSD from working in the hospital during COVID and witnessing the deaths of patients, so she did not want anything having to do with COVID being brought up, including in therapy. So I knew I had to keep my thoughts about what I knew to be true about my condition to myself.

I was approached by Dr. Brown who pulled me aside.

"You need to get ahold of your crying and learn to regulate yourself," she said.

"I'm trying. I just don't know what to do," as I put my face in my hands.

"Stop and calm yourself with an 8-part breath," she replied as she began instructing me on its method.

WTH! I'm a yoga and meditation instructor who teaches others about breathing techniques! She doesn't understand I've tried, and it doesn't work!

I went along with her and followed her instructions just to appease her. I didn't know what else to do.

***

At a therapy session, I couldn't process my feelings. Teri took great offense to that and accused me of holding my feelings inside. I then brought up what I felt had happened to me was due to the vaccine. Teri blew up.

"I'm not going to listen to this!" she screamed as she ran out of the room.

Shortly after Dr. Brown and Teri developed a closer relationship. Dr. Brown would arrive early in the morning to the home, and the two of them would sit outside alone eating breakfast. They also sat around the pool by themselves in the afternoon when the pool was off limits to the rest of us. The other women began to talk about the inappropriateness of what was happening but was afraid to bring it up because of Teri's volatility and bullishness towards me.

Teri also became a problem for the administration staff. She knew how many nurses were required to be present at the home, and the home was lacking the required amount. Teri was given permission by Dr. Brown to go into a private room for a couple nights with her iPad where she called her husband and instructed him on how to call the authorities who oversaw treatment homes such as where we were staying.

Within the next couple days, top administrators of the treatment center showed up and had meetings with Teri over her complaints, which meetings were somewhat heated.

The day after the meetings ended, Teri was given a letter of reprimand and probationary terms to initial and sign.

Teri also told staff to keep me away from her, so I would sit by myself outside on one side of the patio while the others sat on the other side doing their vaping. Teri would constantly chide me from across the patio.

One day Dr. Brown opened the sliding glass window of her office which is where the ladies were sitting. I saw Dr. Brown stick her head out the window and mouth something to Teri.

I then heard Teri say in a loud voice, "She's right there," and pointed to me. This told me that Dr. Brown was possibly revealing confidential information about me. I decided to go into the house and to her office and knocked on her door.

"I hope you're not revealing confidentiality about me. I just heard what Teri said," I told her.

"What are you talking about? I didn't say anything about you! You better get things straight!" she exclaimed.

I walked away feeling distrustful and defeated.

***

It came time for Margie, my roommate, to leave the facility. We all gathered in the therapy room and wished her well.

The following day a new young gal was admitted. Her name was Selina. She was in her early 20s, heavyset, and styled herself as a lot of that generation did with tight shorts and a short top with her belly showing and had lots of beautiful long black curls. We learned Selina was three months pregnant with her first child and would not reveal who the father of the child was.

Selina would be rooming with me. Once she was introduced to everyone, she was brought upstairs and began unpacking her clothes and put them away in the unused drawers of the dresser we shared and put her toiletries away on her side of the bathroom.

I asked Selina, "When do you usually go to sleep?" and, "Are you okay to sleep with the lights off?" trying to accommodate her in the best way I could.

Selina responded, "Usually around 9:00," and, "It's good to turn the lights off."

She seemed friendly enough, and from our first encounter, I saw no issues. As a mother of young adult children myself, I felt I wanted to be there for her as a mother figure if she needed it.

As the days went on, I noticed Selina taking about five showers throughout the day and in the middle of the night. She also washed her clothes constantly, which upset Teri and Brenda.

"You know we have a drought! You need to wait until you have a full load to wash clothes!" said Brenda.

Selina just walked away and continued her routine. I would have to use the other restroom since she was occupying ours most of the time.

In the early morning, we would wake up to loud rap music coming from YouTube TV downstairs that Selina had turned on. That was difficult for me because of my heightened sensitivity.

One evening Brenda was sitting at the kitchen table

eating some freshly made popcorn. Selina came into the kitchen and asked Brenda if she could have some of her popcorn.

Brenda said, "There's microwave popcorn in the cupboard."

Selina looked curiously at Brenda. "I don't know how to use a microwave."

Brenda then showed Selina how to make the popcorn in the microwave.

Selina also had a habit of leaving her dirty dishes on the sink, so she was told that she needed to wash off her dishes and put them in the dishwasher after eating. She seemed to have no idea how to clean up after herself nor how to do basic household tasks.

One evening all of us women except Selina were gathered around the table outside (of course, me at one end and Teri at the other) when Teri began telling us that Selina was schizophrenic and couldn't take her medications because of the pregnancy. She also informed us that Selina lived a very high lifestyle in Beverly Hills with her mother and siblings where maids did all the work for the family. We also learned from Teri that Selina had come from UCLA psych ward and that her family had taken her there while they went vacationing in Greece.

"My concern is, if she is schizophrenic and not taking her meds, is she dangerous here?" questioned Teri. "Plus, how is she going to be able to take care of a baby if she can't even take care of herself?"

Brenda replied, "Oh, yeah, plus, Lynette, you're

rooming with her."

The conversation continued, and we all just seemed to leave things as they were, although I was keeping what was said in the back of my mind.

A few nights later, as Selina was walking up the stairs, I decided I was going to turn in for the night. I got up off the couch downstairs and headed towards the stairway. As I turned to walk up the stairs, Selina yelled from the top of the stairs, "Stop following me!"

"I'm not following you! I'm going to bed," I responded.

Conveniently, one of the night workers happened to be in the area and witnessed the whole incident.

I walked back down the few steps and into the office with the worker.

"I'm not comfortable being in the same room with Selina," I told her.

She replied, "Let me make some phone calls."

I went outside and sat with the ladies. Teri was even somewhat protective of me at this point.

About an hour later, the worker came outside and told me to move to another room at least for that night.

The next day Selina was picked up and taken back to UCLA psych ward.

***

After the two-week period of no contact with anyone outside the facility, I was finally able to have 30-minute phone calls. I called Dan, Kelli, Bryce, and some friends. Dan also would come visit on a weekend when the schedule allowed for visitation, and we were able to spend a few hours together. The backyard was arranged for each of us to have privacy with our family members.

The first visit when I saw Dan for the first time since being dropped off in Costa Mesa, we took each other in our arms and cried. We both were at a loss for where things were going from here. Dan was intent on moving to Florida thinking that once I got there, I would suddenly get better. I couldn't imagine moving to Florida, let alone anywhere else, as my fears were overwhelming. I lost all motivation to do anything which was frustrating because I had always been a go-getter and an adventurer. I know now that it was the brain damage that caused that. As I have since learned through my experience, the simple things we do in life a healthy brain is responsible for. The desire to eat, to choose what to wear, likes and dislikes, the feeling of being clean after a nice shower, engaging with people, feeling any kind of positive emotion, and even the will to live are just a few of the things we take for granted that certain parts of the brain control. I wasn't comfortable in my own skin. I was just a shell.

**

One morning I walked outside and saw Brenda sitting by herself on the grass. I went over to where she was and sat down on the grass close by.

Brenda began talking to me. "You know, you don't belong here. Nobody wants you here. Teri doesn't even want to be around you. I know it's hard to hear, but I'm being honest with you. Your crying and neediness make it hard for us who are trying to recover from our own issues. You are different than the rest of us. I really do think you could be right that it was the vaccine."

As difficult as it was to hear, I responded, "I'm so sorry for everything. Thank you for being frank with me. I am just so afraid I'll try to kill myself again."

"Well, there should be someplace that deals with this. Maybe you should research and find a place to help you," Brenda said.

"Yeah. There is a place in Florida that I hope will work. I just have to get myself there," I replied.

***

As the days went on, Teri became more and more cruel. She constantly made snide comments.

One afternoon we were working on laptops that were provided to each of us to look up follow-up outpatient treatment centers and line up psychiatrists and therapists.

So, I'm supposed to spend months more of my time in places like this when I'm not getting one bit better?

I knew I wasn't going to continue with this type of treatment. I had already been five weeks in the outpatient treatment center the year before with no ability to process plus two psych wards and another treatment center besides this one in which I was already four weeks out. I did make appointments with the psychiatrist I had been seeing and with Katie, my therapist.

Out of the blue, Teri began yelling at me for talking on the phone with my therapist's office as I was instructed to do. It was constant bullying by her. Two of the other ladies went along with her I'm sure for fear of being targeted as I was.

***

A new patient showed up a few days later. Her name was Julie. She was a pleasant lady, probably in her early 40s. While the rest of the ladies were swimming in the pool, I was sitting outside the fenced-in pool, and Julie came and sat down across from me. She began explaining why she was at the facility. She then asked me why I was there. Trying to answer honestly, I responded, "Well, I know it's from the COVID-19 vaccine, and I was hoping meds and therapy would help me." We conversed a bit more and then went about our day.

When visiting day came along, Dan and I were sitting outside with each other sharing a sandwich. A lady who worked in administration walked over to us and handed me a paper.

"This is a contract. I need you to read and sign it agreeing to the statements on there," she said and walked away.

Dan and I read it over. It was putting me on probation because I brought up the word "vaccine." I began to cry. "I can't believe this, Dan. I just want to go home with you."

"You need to finish this out, Lynette. Also, we are moving everything up to Lake Arrowhead in the next two days, and I think it's better to wait till we're there," Dan explained. I knew he was right. The moving caused my nervous system to flare up and thus would begin the tremors and convulsions.

"Okay, honey," as I continued to cry.

I signed the paper.

What else am I going to deal with? God, I know there's a reason why I am going through such Hell. Give me strength, Lord!"

***

About five weeks into the program, all six of us, including a staff member, took a trip to the farmers' market. We could bring our own money or a credit card to purchase whatever we wanted as long as it was an approved item. Tokens needed to be purchased with the credit card in order to buy anything at the farmers' market, so I bought five dollars' worth of tokens. I bought some sweet potatoes thinking I could make some for one of our dinners.

Sam saw some sourdough bread and expressed her interest in it but didn't have any money. I offered to buy her a loaf, but about that time the other ladies were ready to go to the mall. We drove to the mall and walked around for a time.

When everyone was tired of walking the mall and ready to leave, the staff member said we had about a half an hour of time left before we needed to be back to the house, so Sam asked me if I would still buy her a loaf of sourdough bread. I said, "Sure!" Brenda also heard us speaking about it and told the staff member that we needed to go back to the farmers' market.

As we were driving back to the farmers' market, Teri began ranting about my wasting her time because of my wanting to go back to the market.

I said, "We're going back to buy some sourdough bread for Sam!"

She continued with her nasty remarks as we continued on to the farmers' market and then back to the house.

***

The next day was our day for therapy when we all gathered in the make-shift garage.

Dr. Brown instructed us, "I want each of you to tell the group how you are feeling today."

Sam began to answer as I was contemplating whether or not to open my mouth at all since I did not want to deal with Teri's spitefulness.

Trina, a new patient and my new roommate, followed Sam in expressing her thoughts and feelings. Teri then followed Trina after which Julie spoke. Then it came to my turn. I decided not to reveal my inner thoughts and just said, "Nothing has changed."

Teri quickly responded, "You're just sitting there

being stupid!"

"Fuck off, Teri!" I yelled. Everyone in the room, including Dr. Brown opened their eyes wide, and all began screaming at me at the same time Trina jumped up and ran out of the room crying.

"How dare you say that, Lynette!" said Dr. Brown.

You've got to be kidding me! This is a therapy group! They've never heard the "F" word before? Seems like Dr. Brown has not run a real therapy group that gets true feelings out! This is preposterous!

Dr. Brown halted the therapy group.

As soon as I had the chance, I called Kelli who got Dan on a 3-way call, and I told them I'm coming home.

"This is bullshit!" I said.

They began to see what I had been telling them all along, and Dan said he would drive right over to pick me up.

I approached Dr. Brown in her office.

"Dan is coming to pick me up," I told her.

Dr. Brown replied, "You will need to sign a paper that says you are leaving against therapeutic advice. And he won't be able to pick you up until tomorrow."

I was not happy having to wait until the next day, but I accepted it and called Dan about the change of plans.

Later that evening I signed a few discharge papers in order to receive my items back and began packing to leave the next morning.

***

The following morning, I heard the doorbell ring. One of the staff opened the door and greeted Dan. I picked up my suitcase and walked out of the house in which I had been staying for five weeks.

Dr. Brown followed me outside, and we said our goodbyes. Dan and I walked to our RAV4, and we headed on the 2-hour trip to Lake Arrowhead.

As we drove the L.A. freeways, I looked out the window pondering.

I still have no idea where life is leading me. Living in total uncertainty. My health, my home, my whole life.

Chapter 20

Lake Arrowhead is a quaint town in the San Bernardino mountains that reminds me of a little Austrian town. It has a large private lake for boating and fishing that is strictly managed for homeowners only.

We pulled into the garage of the cabin that my aunt and uncle so kindly allowed us to rent until I was ready for the move to Florida.

As we walked in the front door, Miss Kitty Mitty sauntered towards me. I picked her up and held her as I cried.

I then went up the stairs with my suitcase and unpacked my clothes. Kelli had ordered a far-infrared sauna that was recommended by Dr. Arredondo. Hopefully, that would relieve some of the symptoms along with taking ice baths.

Here I am in Lake Arrowhead, and everyone is waiting for me to say the word to move to Florida. We have a home there waiting for us. But I'm no better than I was before. I can't think right. Time and space are totally off. I'm emotionally frightened to go anywhere. All I can do is live moment to moment, All I can do is survive.

The mornings were the most difficult. Outside the windows were beautiful pine trees from which I should have been able to feel beauty inside my heart. Instead, it was fear.

I would get out of bed and go downstairs and make

myself muesli, fruit, and yogurt with decaf tea. Then I would sit in the sauna for 30 minutes and take a cold bath to calm my tremors.

Within a week Kelli flew in from Hawaii and rented a car to stay with me while Dan would go play softball. Kelli would work online during the day and study for the CPA exam at night. My days were basically just sitting outside on the deck or taking a short walk.

I still had the order for blood tests from Dr. Villa, so I finally went to the lab and had 14 vials of blood drawn for my follow-up telemed appointment in the middle of August.

During the three weeks in Lake Arrowhead, I had bouts of crying and threatening my life, even attempting to jump out of the car at times. I just wanted everything to end.

Then came the day of my appointment with Dr. Villa. Kelli and I anxiously waited for the Facetime phone call. Finally, the ringing of the phone sitting on the table in front of us, we could see Dr. Villa on the screen.

"Hi, Lynette!" said Dr. Villa.

"Hi, Dr. Villa. My daughter Kelli is here, too," I said.

Dr. Villa began reviewing the lab results. Most of the standard tests were in the normal range. Then she came to the tests for COVID-19 and the other results.

"It shows you never had COVID. Your cytokines are very high, and you are off the chart for Epstein-Barr virus. This is definitely from the COVID shot," Dr. Villa informed us.

"Dr. Villa, please bring my mom back," Kelli pleaded.

"Lynette, you need to come to Florida. You're not going to get any help in California," she said.

"Okay. " I agreed with reluctance in my voice.

As soon as we said our goodbyes and hung up the phone, Kelli make a call to Dan who was on his way back up the mountain from softball and said, "Dad, you're leaving for Florida tomorrow. Mom and I will fly out in three days."

Dan, surprised, said, "Okay. You're taking the cat."

Here started the debate! "No way! You're taking the cat! I'm not taking Mom and the cat, too!" Kelli adamantly responded.

Kelli then purchased first class airline tickets for us to fly from Ontario to Orlando three days later and made a room reservation for us to stay the night before close to the Ontario airport. She also made room reservations for Dan's three nights traveling across the country.

Dan pulled into the driveway a few hours later, and all three of us began packing up the SUV, kitty litter and all.

The next day we said our goodbyes, and off Dan went to our new place in Florida.

The next few days Kelli worked, and we took walks in the early evenings by the lake.

I also called Aviv Clinic and paid for the testing that was required before treatment would begin.

The day came to leave Southern California. We drove down the mountain to the hotel, checked in, ate dinner, and went to bed to be up for our morning flight to Orlando.

Chapter 21

The flight to Orlando was unremarkable, although being in first class was memorable. We exited the plane at dusk. Dan was waiting for us outside baggage claim. We picked up our luggage off the conveyor belt and met Dan outside. After loading our gear, we drove out of the airport terminal.

I soon began feeling anxious and out of control

"Stop the car!" I yelled. "Go into this parking lot! I have to get out!"

Dan drove into the hotel parking lot I had pointed to and found a row of empty slots and parked our SUV. I quickly got out of the car and started crying uncontrollably.

I feel as if I'm going to come out of my skin!

As Dan and Kelli approached me, I screamed, "Why did you make me come here?" as I lunged towards Dan ready to hit him. I was totally out of control.

Dan grabbed my arms and Kelli yelled, "Mom, stop!"

"I hate you!" I screamed as I wept. "I can't do this!"

Take me, God! Take me! This is too much for me!

Kelli kept reassuring me, "Mom, you are going to get better at Aviv."

"Yes, Lynette. Give it a chance," Dan added.

In time I finally calmed down, and we went on our way to our new home in The Villages.

I now know the damage to the brain was responsible for all of this unusual behavior. There is something in the brain that allows us to tolerate any kind of change, wanted or not. That part of my brain was shut down. Every little change was overwhelming. The major change of going from Ontario to Orlando to begin a new life was extreme.

As we drove up the driveway of our new home, Dan opened the garage door with the automatic opener, and all I could see were boxes stacked on each side of the garage.

How am I ever going to unpack this and make a new home for us?

We settled in for our first night living in Florida.

***

As the days went on, I would unpack in times I wasn't feeling overwhelmed. Dan would unpack when I wasn't in the garage to watch. Kelli worked during the days. We would eat breakfast at home and have dinner out at restaurants at Sumter Landing and Brownwood Square. Cody's became a favorite restaurant of ours during that time.

When we ate out at restaurants, I would watch the people around the squares.

Why can't I enjoy life like everyone else around me? What is wrong with me that I've lost all the good feelings I used to have?

I was also going to Dr. Villa's office two times a week getting Vitamin C and glutathione IVs, which took four to five hours for such treatment until I began testing at Aviv Clinic.

***

The week of testing at Aviv Clinics in the Villages, Florida, finally came. The first day consisted of blood tests, a physical exam, and a spirometry exam. The second day was spent in the lab where I received an MRI, SPECT scan, and chest x-ray. The third day was filled with an interview by the neuropsychologist on my history and a cognitive assessment.

Dr. Miller, the neuropsychologist, asked me about my family history, a history of mental illness, and whether I had any head injuries in my life. I was very open about my childhood and the fact that therapy had helped me out tremendously. I also told him about a concussion I received when I fell off a bike at five years of age. I also explained how everything had changed once I got the COVID-19 vaccine, the suicidal feelings I had, the attempt on my life, and the treatment centers and psych wards.

Dr. Miller then asked the question, "What is your goal here with Aviv Clinics?"

"I just want to feel some enjoyment in life again," I replied.

Waiting for the results was nerve-wracking. The fear in my head of not being accepted into the program overwhelmed me for the week and a half before my pre-assessment for the results of all the testing.

What if they deny me because of the suicide attempt? Maybe they will think I'm too much of a risk to let me be in the program. Oh, God, I'm not going to make it in! This is my last resort! Then what will I do?

The day of my pre-assessment I walked into the clinic and checked in with Sallie at the front desk.

"Just have a seat, Lynette. Dr. Alvarez will be right with you," Sallie said.

Within five minutes Dr. Alvarez came out into the lobby and greeted me.

"Hi, Lynette! Let's go into my office," he said.

We walked through a large black door and went down the hallway into his office. As I sat down in the chair in front of his desk, Dr. Alvarez said, "Boy, you sure spilled the beans to Dr. Miller! There was a question about you. But I'm the one who makes the final decision, and you're in."

Thank you, God! I made it in!

Dr. Alvarez went over all the testing, which basically was normal except for the SPECT scan.

"This is how we know what you have. See these blue forks here? That's damage to your frontal lobe which means you have long COVID," he explained to me.

I knew it! And previous antibody tests showed I never had the COVID virus. It is from the vaccine!

He continued, "There's also some damage to the basal ganglia.

"Before you start, Dr. Miller wants some medical records."

I left Dr. Alvarez' office feeling vindicated proving all my naysayers wrong. The realization that I actually had brain damage was somewhat satisfying because it meant I wasn't going crazy after all.

I'm not crazy! I'm not becoming my mom and getting Alzheimer's. I actually have brain damage. No wonder the symptoms are like I've never felt before!

I was given a list of items that Dr. Miller needed which were the hospitalization records, a meeting with my counselor in California, and a meeting with him, Dan, and me.

After fulfilling the requested conditions, I was scheduled to start diving in the chamber at 10:00 a.m. Monday through Friday for sixty dives. The term "diving" is used because physiologically it is similar to scuba diving in that it is breathing gases while being subject to higher-than-normal atmospheric pressures.

I chose the 10:00 a.m. dive because a new friend Donna I had met through our neighbors Kim and Scott was diving at that time.

Chapter 22

The first day of my treatment at Aviv, I awoke and donned the cotton t-shirt and sweatpants that were required to be worn while in the chamber. No jewelry, no makeup, and no fragrance which I hadn't bothered to wear for the whole year and a half up to this point anyway. Such requirements were the safety protocol to avoid anything flammable in the chamber. We were all assigned an Aviv bracelet with a microchip in it that had our personal information for scanning when we had our vitals taken each day before the dive and to open a locker in the locker room.

***

As I got into the passenger seat with Dan at the wheel on our way to Aviv, about a 20-minute drive, I watched out the window wondering where this first day was taking me in my life knowing this was my last hope.

Just do what you have to do every step of the way and see where it leads.

Dan pulled up to the curb outside the Advanced Medical Center building, and we said our goodbyes. I walked into the clinic and checked in with Sallie at the front desk. I had arrived in plenty of time to go down the hallway to a little café and get something to eat.

I opened the large, heavy doors to the Standard Café and noticed a few college-age adults behind the counter. Looking at the homemade goods, I noticed some gluten-free energy bites in a jar.

Just perfect! Something healthy and fresh!

"I'll have a decaf cappuccino with almond milk and sugar-free vanilla, please, and two of the energy bites," I ordered.

After waiting for a few minutes, the young lady handed me a paper bag with the energy bites and the decaf cappuccino. As I looked down at the cappuccino, I noticed a heart swirled in the foam.

How sweet!

I thanked the young lady and walked out of the café and back to the clinic where I found a seat in the lobby with a table in front of it with a local Villages newspaper. I tried reading some of the newspaper while having breakfast and noticed the usual issue of not being able to focus or retain much.

Soon Donna walked into the clinic and over to where I was sitting. As she sat down on the chair next to mine, she said, "Well, are you ready?"

"I sure am. We need to get our vitals taken at 9:30, right?" I asked.

"Yes. Then we can go into the lounge to put on our booties before we're called into the chamber." She said.

"Okay. How many dives have you done?" I asked Donna.

"I'm on my 13th dive," Donna replied.

We chatted for a few more minutes before going to the back to have our vitals taken.

As I sat down in the seat with the blood pressure gauge and other instruments, a very pretty young blonde lady in dark blue scrubs came to my chair and said, "Hi, Lynette! I'm Brittany. Welcome to your first day!"

As she proceeded to scan my bracelet and take my vitals, she said, "We are here any time you need anything."

"Thank you," I replied.

Donna and I then proceeded to the lounge where we put on our booties and waited until we were called into the chamber. As we were chatting, nine more clients walked into the lounge, helped themselves to bananas, water, or tea, and sat down.

At approximately 9:55 a.m. a male nurse opened the door to the lounge and exclaimed, "It's time!"

We all got up from our seats and walked out of the lounge into one of four chambers.

It looks just like an airplane!

Cheryl, another client, said to me, "Look at the iPad in front of the seats to find your name on it so you know where you're sitting."

Aviv Clinics is the only HBoT in the world that has iPads or any electronics in the chambers. Electronics are flammable in an HBoT chamber. The iPads were specially made for Aviv chambers so that clients can do brain exercises while going through the 2-hour session. The research behind this is to stress the area of the brain where the stem cells will go to regenerate damaged cells and make new, healthy cells.

As it turned out, I would be sitting next to Cheryl. She is a very attractive woman from New York City who was being treated at Aviv for multiple sclerosis, although one would not be able to visibly see that she had such a debilitating condition.

I sat down in my nicely upholstered chair and looked around at everyone in the chamber. Donna was sitting catty-corner to me.

Suddenly the doors slid closed reminding me of the sound of the jail doors closing where I worked some years before.

The nurse's voice came across the chamber, "It's time to decompress!"

The next ten minutes were spent plugging our noses and blowing out our ears or cracking open our jaws to relieve the pressure. A stick of gum was passed around beforehand to help, too. We all conversed with one another as we made our funny faces.

"Time to put on the mask," the nurse said after the ten minutes of decompression was up.

We all put our personally fitted masks over our noses and mouths and clicked the strap so the mask was snug. The nurse came by and turned on our pressure so that we were now breathing 100% medical-grade oxygen versus the 21% we normally breathe.

I don't feel anything different from normally breathing. Hmmmmmm...interesting.

I pulled the iPad in front of me up to eye level and began my personally prescribed 30 to 40 minutes of brain exercises to help stimulate the areas in my brain that are damaged, i.e., the frontal lobe and basal ganglia.

After twenty minutes of being on 100% oxygen, the nurse directed us to take off the mask for five minutes. During this time we could get up and stretch, drink some water, or make conversation with each other. After five minutes, the mask goes back on for another twenty minutes. This 20-minute-on-5-minute-off protocol repeats four times during the two hours while being in the chamber. See https://mdpi.com/2218-273X/10/6/958/htm for the study on the research behind this protocol.

The last ten minutes consists of decompressing before exiting the chamber.

***

That first week I would have no physical therapy, nutrition guidance, or neuropsychology follow-ups, but those appointments would begin the second week. I was also given counseling appointments for the PTSD and distress I was having. All the appointments were held inside the clinic. All personnel were at the clinic all day every day. Appointments with any of the Aviv personnel were easy to make and usually within two weeks' time, if not sooner. The personnel are constantly roaming the clinic and are happy to speak with clients at a moment's notice as long as they weren't scheduled for an appointment.

The atmosphere at the Aviv Clinic is warm and welcoming. All the personnel are very positive and caring. The personnel consist of anything from a concierge to an event planner to all the medical professionals. I have never met a group of professionals who were more positive and caring. It is truly an outstanding and phenomenal place and is like no other medical facility in the world.

Chapter 23

The treatment period had its ups and downs. Healing was slow for me and didn't clearly come to fruition until after the sixty treatments where it really took off.

There were times when I felt as if I were going backwards. At those few times, I sought out a nurse practitioner who I felt was one of the most knowledgeable people in the medical field I had ever met and reported what I was feeling.

"Roma, I feel as if I'm going backwards," I complained. "My head feels so much pressure."

Roma responded, "That's a good thing! That means that your brain is really working hard!"

"How about the nerves in my body?" I asked.

"There's a myelin sheath around the nerves that the stem cells will also repair. Think of these three months as boot camp. There is a lot of healing after you finish your treatment," he advised.

As much as my impatience didn't want to hear it, his words gave me hope then and future times when I was feeling the same way.

***

As time went on, our dive mates would finish their sixty dives. Aviv made it a graduation, and staff stood outside the chamber on the last dive with pom-poms and signs. Family members and friends would show up with flowers and cupcakes.

America's Mighty Warriors was sponsoring a number of military veterans for PTSD, traumatic brain injury, and a few with Long COVID. Our dive had three Navy Seals, a Vietnam veteran, and an Air Force veteran. It was fascinating to get to know them and hear their stories.

One thing many of us with Long COVID and the military veterans struggled with were suicidal thoughts, if not attempts, were a huge factor. It was comforting to know I was not the only one who felt this way. I know now that it was the part of the brain that was damaged that caused that.

Being able to be with others struggling with Long COVID and other conditions was very helpful. We would share what things worked for each other; for example, a breathing practice or a certain supplement or medication. On the weekends some of us would meet for dinner. I am ever so grateful for all my dive mates. There is a special bond we share, no matter the reason we were at Aviv. Every one of you will always be in my heart.

During the treatment I began going back to the gym where I would do a Synergy class or lift weights and practice yoga on the turf. Some of my dive mates I would also see at the gym.

***

I am one who loves to take baths rather than showers. My bathtub in California was a sanctuary for me until I got injured. Not only is the bath calming for me, but

I also do some yoga poses while in the bath to warm up some muscles and joints and work out the stiffness most of us feel first thing in the morning, especially as we age.

The house we purchased in The Villages did not have a bath in the master bathroom which became a huge disappointment very soon after we moved in. The house was also very small and was what our daughter Kelli referred to as a "bachelor pad," if that gives an idea of what we were living in at the time. As time went on and my brain began getting clearer, I realized the house was not one I would be happy in long term. Of course, at the time we purchased it, I was in no shape to choose any kind of living space. I did not have my normal desires or intuition to properly pick out a home that, once I was able-brained, I would be able to feel comfortable.

I questioned a realtor as we drove to some of the new areas being sold in The Villages.

"Are there bathtubs in any of the master bathrooms?" I asked.

He replied, "No. This is a senior community, and there's concern over falling, so there are only showers."

Damn! I guess I'll have to deal with that.

Well, lo and behold, as I was looking in the newspaper, there were two homes with a bathtub in the master bathroom! I showed Dan the paper, and he immediately called our realtor Shane.

That day we drove by one of the homes for sale in

the paper and liked that it was on a cul-de-sac. The neighbors were gathered in a driveway, drinks in hand, and waved us down, so we stopped and talked with them.

What a friendly bunch! Very welcoming! Well, this is a sign!

Within the next few days, Shane met us at the home. As we walked in the doorway, the first view I had was of a large open family room with high ceilings and a view into the lanai and past that a golf course with a lake. The colors of blue painted walls with white crown molding gave it a coastal flair. It was perfect! Although I still didn't have my full brain with me, I just knew it was the house for us. It was spacious with three bedrooms and two bathrooms, the master with the bathtub with jets. Turning back from looking out at the backyard, I noticed a beautifully painted mural of a Mediterranean scene over the dining room area.

Dan immediately said, "I'm buying you this house."

Dan made all the phone calls to the lenders, got all the paperwork together, and had everything set up for our signing of escrow papers within the week. In thirty days' time we had movers packing up the untouched boxes from the first house to go to our new home.

We knew we needed to shop for furniture, so the hunt began. I still had to force myself to shop and pick out furnishings. I had always wanted a home with coastal décor, so I chose a master bedroom set with the Nantucket style and beach décor for the family room and dining room. I shopped at a local Home Goods for lamps and ocean décor for our home. After all, we were an hour and a half away from both coastlines.

Still diving, I did notice small differences. I was able to start unpacking a box in the garage. One of our new neighbors walked her dog around the neighborhood and would stop to say good morning. A week went by with each day of her greeting us when she commented, "Lynette, you've been at that same box ever since you moved in." That clued me in to how difficult it still was to unpack. So different from how I used to be such an efficient organizer.

***

During the treatment I still had times where suicidal feelings came up, brain pressure, neuropathy, fast heartbeats, but I knew I was improving slowly but surely because of gaining the little motivation to shop and unpack. I also began cooking and juicing Florida oranges. But I knew I had to be patient to (cross my fingers) see dramatic results.

Then came December 22, 2022, when I had my 60th and final dive.

Gosh, today is my last day, and I'm still not as clear as I want to be. I need to be patient for the stem cells to really do their job!

As we finished decompressing the last ten minutes of the dive, all my dive mates got up and formed a bridge for me to walk under as "Congratulations" and "Great job" were cheered.

I walked out of the chamber and immediately saw

Dan with a bouquet of flowers among the group of Aviv staff, some with pom-poms, shouting, "Congratulations, Lynette!" I stood in front of the chamber and looked at everyone as I told them, "Thank you all! I never would have made it without you!"

As I walked up to Dan, I noticed tears welling up in his eyes as he hugged me tightly and then handed me the flowers.

I walked around to each person, and we hugged one another for my final day.

***

The next week was the Christmas holidays where Dan and I went to Kelli and Jeff's in Jacksonville to celebrate with Steve and Angie, Jeff's parents. I had decided to take on my usual task pre-vaccine of cooking Christmas prime rib and all the fixings. Things were still a blur, but I pulled it off. I knew I had to function as if life were back to normal. I still lacked the clarity and quickness and emotional connection I had three Christmases before this.

Kelli was nine months pregnant with our first grandson, so all four of us grandparents were eagerly awaiting his birth knowing it would be any day. We had a nice Christmas all together and even played a few games.

Dan and I left home the day after Christmas.

Then we got the call on the afternoon of the 31st of December that Kelli was in labor. We waited by the phone until we got the news that our first grandson was born that evening of New Year's Eve. Dan and I were so excited. I say, "excited" for what I could feel at the time.

Dan and I both said to each other, "We're going to have a party every year!"

Dan and I hopped in the car and drove back to Kelli and Jeff's house to help the new parents on their first day home from the hospital. We arrived at the front door and gave our congratulations and hugs to Jeff as Kelli was with the baby in the nursery. I walked into the nursery seeing Kelli changing her new baby boy that they had been through so much to have.

"Mom, sit in the rocking chair," Kelli said.

Kelli picked up her precious little one and put him in my arms.

Oh, my gosh, he's perfect! His tiny fingers and toes, his cute little nose, his adorable cheeks, and he smells so good! What a miracle from God! It's so nice to finally feel an inkling of joy. I know this is the beginning of a new life for all of us.

Chapter 24

After a few days of helping out the new mommy and daddy and holding our grandson, we drove home. I concentrated on spending my days following a regimen of eating healthfully, doing the recommended gym workouts, planting roses, gardenias, agapanthus, and milk week for our butterflies.

My mornings are my favorite time to spend in the lanai with the large open windows where I have a breakfast of muesli, yogurt and berries and drink coffee and pray to my God. At that time in the mornings, I still lacked a lot of the emotional connection but kept my belief in practicing faith in something much bigger than any of us can fathom.

One morning about two and a half weeks after finishing treatment, I sat down with my decaf and breakfast and looked out the window as I had been doing since moving into our new home. I couldn't believe my eyes.

Wow! My world is no longer distorted! I can see life as I had for 61 years of my life before the injury! Can this really be happening?

It was then that I definitely knew the treatment was working. Little by little things were coming back. Within a few months I had unpacked all the boxes and organized our home. I began cooking on a regular basis, making grass-fed steaks and grain-fed chicken with organic vegetables. I knew it was important to eat well to keep inflammation down in the body.

Total insomnia was one of the first symptoms I had that April 7, 2021, evening, so I had been on a benzodiazepine in order to sleep. Within two months of finishing the dives, I weaned myself off the medication, and I am able to sleep soundly as I did before without any medication at all. This tells me the area of the brain in control of sleep was damaged. How else could it be explained of two years of no ability to even fall asleep without certain medications?

Also the PTSD and suicidal thoughts are totally gone. I have had depression in my life but never felt truly suicidal like I did for almost two years. It was totally different. I now know there is a place in the brain that is in charge of motivating one to live on a daily basis to, for example, get a beverage to drink or something to eat, shower, or use one's senses to do anything. I have experienced that being gone. I was just surviving.

Neuropathy is no longer an issue. Tinnitus is very mild, sometimes not at all, but I know tinnitus usually never goes away.

My sensitivity to light and sound soon died down, and I have been able to enjoy concerts, watch TV, and be out in the Florida sunshine.

The postural orthostatic tachycardia (POTS) is gone. I now work out doing HIIT workouts at the local Orange Theory five to six times a week at full speed. It is so nice to be able to breathe deeply and know that my pulse rate is working normally.

After the Aviv treatment, I volunteered my services to teach yoga at the clinic which they took me up on. I am also doing meditation workshops for them. I teach yoga at the local gym, too.

Soon after my treatment, I was asked by Aviv to be one of twelve alumni ambassadors where we volunteer in various areas such as attending presentations where we are available to speak with prospective clients about our experiences at Aviv. I also make myself available to present clients who may be struggling to give them a little extra support. I have gained a tremendous education through my work with Aviv on so many aspects related to the human body and health. I am so grateful to Aviv for using me to help heal others as I have been healed. It gives me a great sense of purpose as well.

In October 2023 I met three girlfriends from California in Rome. I flew by myself to Rome and checked into our Airbnb and spent the afternoon visiting the ancient sites of the famous city. My friends arrived the next day. We boarded a cruise ship for Corsica, the Italian Riviera, French Riviera, Isle de Mallorca, and debarked in Barcelona, Spain. I never thought I would travel again, let alone to Europe.

Dan and I have been exploring the east side of the country. In April 2024 we drove to Memphis where we stayed two nights. Visiting the location of Martin Luther King's assassination brought me to tears as I remembered as an 8-year-old the devastation people felt on the April 4, 1968, day of a man who gave us all the message of peace, nonviolence, and acceptance of other human beings, no matter the color of our skin. I felt grateful to be able to feel the grief rather than any lack of emotion I had been feeling for almost two years.

We then drove to Nashville and met our friends Lance and Susie. Over the three nights we stayed in

Nashville, we spent a lot of time on Broadway Street where country bands played in every venue along the way. It was great to be able to listen to the music and even have a bourbon or a glass of wine. I had not had alcohol during the time of my injury. Even a slight bit of alcohol did something very strange to my brain that I can't even describe.

Chapter 25

I asked my husband Dan if he would share a bit of his story. He also told me, "We're in this together."

What I went through as Lynette's husband was the worst time of my life. I've been through a divorce, lost my oldest son after dealing with his committing crimes and in and out of prison, witnessed heinous crimes as a law enforcement officer, and was in a shooting with a murder suspect, but nothing compares to what I went through because of Lynette's injury to her brain.

For the 38 years of our marriage, Lynette was a vibrant, fun-loving woman dedicated to our family, her career, fitness, her friends, and she loved adventure. She made sure our house was clean and organized, did the bills, planned all vacations, and made sure we were taken care of. Within a week of taking the second shot, things changed dramatically with the insomnia, complaints of loud ringing in her head and the feeling of pins and needles all over her body, and loss of focus. And it went further downhill from there. Watching her wither away in a couple months' time, the nights of her being awake all night, the drugs she was prescribed for sleep that wouldn't work, the tremors and convulsions, her taking cold baths multiple times during the night, her loss of motivation to do anything, all was very unusual.

The most frightening times came when she would talk about not wanting to live any longer and then finally telling me she needed to go somewhere to get help for feeling suicidal. That was just within the first three months. As time went on, day in and day out, she made attempts on her life, and I helped her to try to find some hope. We were in this together. I was so scared. I didn't know if, when, or where something might happen to her. I felt helpless.

Lynette went to many doctors and still could find no permanent relief. She would cry for hours on end. I didn't know what to do except just be there for her. And I had no idea where our life would be taking us. I felt like we were in the "Twilight Zone."

Our dream of moving to Florida in our retirement years was planned to follow our daughter and son-in-law, and I thought that move might help her, but I didn't understand the gravity of what was happening inside her. She had no ability to do any decision-making about selling the California house and doing what needed to be done to move away. Thankfully, I did get the house sold and, with the help of our daughter, got her to Florida, but not without distress. The uncertainty of life continued in our new place in Florida, but we were fortunate to have found Aviv Clinic right in our backyard.

Once Lynette got her pre-assessment back and was found to have brain damage, it was a relief to finally have an understanding as to the strange symptoms and behavior. When the treatment began, she got herself up every morning and did everything she needed to do at the clinic for the three months. Our children and I knew Aviv was the last chance for her.

I noticed little changes happening within the three months of treatment such as her cooking again, some unpacking, and shopping for furniture and décor for the house. A week and a half after the treatment, our first grandson was born, and that was the first time that I saw her seeming to have some joy.

Within six months to a year after treatment, Lynette regained all the abilities she had before her injury. She is the happy, fun-loving wife that I married 40 years ago and is doing all the activities she was doing before, except she is retired from her career and volunteering helping others afflicted with long COVID, whether from the virus or the vaccine. She is back to her high-intensity fitness training and teaching yoga and meditation. She is loving life again.

I am grateful to Aviv Clinic for saving Lynette's life. I would have spent every dime I had to put her through Aviv in order to be healed. Whenever I see anyone from Aviv, I always tell them, "You saved my wife's life!"

Chapter 26

To explain to anyone what it is like to go through this journey is difficult because it is like nothing anyone has ever experienced. As we see, doctors are misdiagnosing Long COVID, either from the vaccine or the virus, regularly because they have never experienced seeing patients with the myriad of symptoms. Most of us injured look fine from the outside, although many wind up in wheelchairs, feeding tubes, and more. Inside us though we were wiped hollow. Our normal thought process has escaped us. We are overwhelmed by everyday stimulation: sunlight, music, conversation, change. The heart is suddenly beating as if it is coming out of our chest. The body feels like a pin cushion or, worse, we are being stabbed. We are in a state of survival, so we don't care about the minutia in life. We are just doing what we need to do every minute to keep ourselves alive.

Here are a few poems I wrote about my journey:

Awakening to open eyes,
I realize once again the fragility of which I feel,
I lay here convincing myself that in spite of the guttural pain,
I will carry on,
Bringing my knees to my chest gives a sense of security,
Rolling onto my side trying to find a place that lets me know this feeling is not real,
That I don't have to really fight this hard to live the morning,
I close my eyes hoping the brokenness will go away,
To no avail,

I finally sit up and force myself to rise,
As I walk I can feel the house of glass in which I am
abiding,
I have hope for treatment,
But in the meantime telling myself to just live through
moment by moment,
Bringing attention to my family,
For that is the only option,
Praying for healing.

Where did my ego go?
The ego to be human,
It is gone,
Just a shell,
The realm of total humility,
Trying to survive,
No dreams or plans,
Waiting for a miracle,
Or is this my life?

Chapter 27

For my final chapter I want to explore the meaning behind my journey for two years as I try to look at things at a spiritual level.

I have the belief that we are on this Earth to become more spiritual, more connected with something bigger and more profound than anything we can imagine. Call it God, Heaven, eternal life, reincarnation, whatever your belief system is. I am open to it all. I just know there is something beyond this life here. I also believe we reach higher levels of spirituality in a lifetime and that we are spiritual beings living in a material world. Becoming more connected, more spiritual, and truly happy inside is about being humble enough to know oneself deeply by accepting and embracing oneself, flaws and all, knowing why we are here on Earth, and knowing what moves us, so that we can be a light for our own self and others.

For many years in later adulthood, I prayed to reach a higher level of spirituality. From this whole journey, I feel it has brought me to that place of deeper connection and meaning. There are too many things that happened in the two years that not to call it spiritually enlightening would be ignorant. The timing of everything was too coincidental: Our plans to move to the only place in the nation where I was fully healed, only because Kelli and Jeff were transferred back to Florida at the same time; selling our home in California at the top of the market and before interest rates skyrocketed; picking Dr. Villa out of the blue while still in California as my primary doctor; buying our first home across the street from neighbors going through the Aviv treatment; the timing of a new medical breakthrough to treat brain injury.

From the years of therapy I had, I had learned not only about the dysfunction within my own family, but also about different behavioral issues that human beings have from birth or environmental factors. I had worked through most of my childhood issues, but there was one that I was still carrying, a huge issue. I knew that one day if I wanted to have that deeper connection and true happiness that I would have to unleash it. The invisible wound that I had actually was the catalyst that allowed me to release the burden I was carrying. And when it came time to let it go, it seemed to come very naturally for me leaving me with a freedom within that I had never felt before.

My life now is better than I ever imagined. It would not be as fulfilling if I had not gone through what I did. I feel freer than ever to love, be silly, and have fun. The joy of being a grandmother is like nothing else. To be able to be of service and try to bring healing to others' suffering is my mission. I do my best to keep humility, for that is where the soul lies at its deepest. And in the end, I will know I was given a second chance to experience the true meaning of my life.

Lynette's During Treatment and After Photos

During treatment, after vax injury:

After Treatment:

A Word of Thanks

I want to personally mention by name the beautiful beings I am so grateful to for supporting me not only during the darkness, but also those who reached out to me with love and concern after our move to Florida. With love and gratitude for your genuine love and support: I love you all and thank you for your genuine love and support: Dan, Bryce, Kelli, Jeff, Deanna, Dad and Susie, Angie and Steve, Courtney and Brian, Debbie, Pablo and Vicki, Devin, Barb and Phil, Sandy and Tom, Susie and Lance, Lori and Vern, Candi and Randy, Don and Susie, Joan, Laurie, Toni, Mary, Leisha, Deena, Betty, Debbie, Julie and Scott, Jennifer and Brian, Monica and my Claremont Yoga friends, Betty, Michelle and my Pedal Spin friends, Maria, Brenda and Eric, Gina, Samantha, Amalya, Faye, Jazzmin, MacKenzie, Reanna, Donna and Ed, Kim and Scott, Will, Julio, Chris, Nick, Rob, Sherman and Diane, Rick, Danielle, Kim, Amalya, Julia, Nick, Donna, Dragana, Dr. Lisa Forsyth, Lori, Kristin, Jaimie, Lena, Kelly, Natalie, Ana, Lisa, Kathryn, Sheryl, Patty, James, Keller, Dawn, Tri, JC, Dr. Mo, Dr. Cook, Dr. Hadanny, Dr. Miller, Dr. Lowry, Aaron, Roma, Brittany, Debbie, Sallie, John, Tim, Donna, Jason, Cheyenne, Ankita, D'Asia, Joel, and all Aviv staff, Dr. Villa and her staff, Sonia, Cheryl, Lindy, Sean and Patty, Cindy, Mike and Penny, Linda and Bob, Linda, Tom, Jennifer and Lorne, Malia, Barbara, Lynette, Gina, and all Aviv friends, my publisher: Sheila Farr, my wonderful neighbors, and all my friends and supporters from all over the world.

Recommended Reading or Viewing

Aviv Clinic, YouTube

The Long-Haul: My Four-Year Battle to Beat Long-COVID,
ME/CFS, and POTS by Matthew Robinson, PhD

The Pfizer Papers; Edited by Naomi Wolf with Amy Kelly

Canary in a COVID World

The Courage to Face Covid-19; John Leake & Peter A.
McCullough

Cause Unknown; Edward Dowd

Rare Courage; Jodi O'Malley

The COVID-19Vaccine and Beyond; Sally Saxon, J.D.;
Deborah Viglione, M.D.; and James Thorp, M.D.

Medical Medium; Anthony Williams

Resources

Websites:

Anthem BCBS: Providers | Tools, Resources & More | Anthem.com

CDC/COVID Vaccines: Staying Up to Date with COVID-19 Vaccines | COVID-19 | CDC

Full study on post-Covid:
https://www.nature.com/articles/s41598-022-15565-0.

Proposition 47:
The impact of Prop 47 on crime in San Francisco | GrowSF.org

Hyperbaric chamber protocol:
https://mdpi.com/2218-273X/10/6/958/htm

Articles:

Journey, M. L. S., Model, E. T. M. S., Living, H., & Center, M. Tag: COVID-19. (2021).

Murray, P. C. (1987). DTP Vaccine Related Injury: An Examination of Proposed Vaccine Injury Compensation Legislation. *J. Contemp. Health L. & Pol'y*, *3*, 233.

Pierson, B. (2023). California law amazing to curb COVID misinformation blocked by judge. Reuters. https://www.reuters.com/article/health-coronavirus-californiat-law-idUSKBN2FQ2JL

Zachary, S. (2021). A preparation that is used to stimulate the body's immune response against diseases. Epoch Times.

Zilberman-Itskovich S, Catalogna M, Sasson E, Elman-Shina K, Hadanny A, Lang E, Finci S, Polak N, Fishlev G, Korin C, Shorer R, Parag Y, Sova M, Efrati S. Hyperbaric oxygen therapy improves neurocognitive functions and symptoms of post-COVID condition: randomized controlled trial. Sci Rep. 2022 Jul 12;12(1):11252. doi: 10.1038/s41598-022-15565-0. PMID: 35821512; PMCID: PMC9276805.

Zuckerberg, D. M. (2021). Covid-19: Researcher blows the whistle on 19: Researcher blows the whistle on data integrity issues in Pfizer's vaccine trial data integrity issues in Pfizer's vaccine trial. *BMJ*, 375.

Made in United States
Orlando, FL
13 September 2024

51497620R00086